What They Don't Teach You in

Broadcasting

What They Don't Teach You in
Broadcasting

Orji Ogbonnaya Orji, *PhD*
Senior Executive Fellow, Harvard Kennedy School

Safari Books Ltd
Ibadan

Published by
Safari Books Ltd
Ile Ori Detu
1, Shell Close
Onireke
Ibadan.
Email: safarinigeria@gmail.com

Publisher: Chief Joop Berkhout, *OON*
Deputy Publisher: George Berkhout

First Published 2014

ISBN: 978-978-8431-64-0

Dedication

To my mother, Oyidia Orji (Nnenne), who taught me the value of hardwork and how to face challenges of life without depending on anyone. Nnenne's hard choices, commitment and efforts, laid the foundation.

To my dear wife, Essie, for being a wonderful friend, partner and pillar of support. I cannot forget my wonderful children: Nnenna, Orji O. Orji Jnr. and Chinatu; our love and commitment to one another will continue to shape our bright future.

Contents

Acknowledgements

To God Almighty for His mercies and grace! I wish to thank my friend, Ogechukwu Ajuzie, who worked closely with me to develop the structure and scope of this book. I am also grateful to my colleague, Hilary Enenche, who carefully proofread the manuscript; Oluremi Bello, who served as research assistant; and my staff, Ogechi Nwobia, for all her valued contributions. I cannot forget my nephews, Adam and Tochukwu, and my niece, Ndidi, I appreciate your various support at every stage of this work. I am also grateful to my in-law and good friend, Emma Igbo, for his valued advise at important stages of this work. I wish to thank my publishers, Safari Books Limited, Ibadan, under the leadership of Chief Joop Berkhout, his son, George and his Publishing Manager, Moyofade Ipadeola. I cherish your professionalism, support and industry.

I am also grateful to the Director General of Federal Radio Corporation of Nigeria, Dr. Lada Salihu, for his support. Finally, my appreciation goes to all former and present Management and Staff of the Federal Radio Corporation of Nigeria for the opportunities and their friendship.

Foreword

One of the many problems the media in Nigeria and developing nations contend with is the absence of current books and journals written by practitioners whose experiences were based on our level of development, existing regulations and local environments. This problem has continued to frustrate the development of the profession in this part of the world. This is because a good number of media professionals who have gained tremendous experience and exposure in the profession, based on our development challenges, level of technology and culture and tradition hardly write books to share their knowledge with the next generation. It is therefore sad that many accomplished journalists and broadcasters die with all the knowledge and experience acquired without any form of documentation for posterity.

I am aware that it is very difficult to find books authored by a popular Nigerian journalist or broadcaster in use in our Higher Institutions of learning. As a result, the media industry and educational institutions have little or no relevant materials with which they can advance the course of learning and research. Under the ugly circumstances, what we find common are books and journals from foreign journalists and practitioners whose experiences have very little bearing on the training and working needs of our local environment in Nigeria and other developing countries. This is worrisome, considering the knowledge gap that exists between the theoretical aspects taught in schools and practical experience in the field when actual work begins.

The broadcast media appears to be the worst hit by this scarcity of books and journals written by professionals whose reputations and accomplishments, we are familiar with. It is against this background that I wish to commend Dr. Orji Ogbonnaya Orji for what I consider a timely intervention. I am aware that many in his stead, endowed with experience, exposure and intellect would rather have written praise singing books on political officer holders; a common phenomenon in our society today for purposes of making quick money.

Orji's decision to document his vast experience in the media over the years for the benefit of teaching and learning in our educational institutions is not only commendable but worthy of emulation. I am however not quite surprised at the author's resilience, industry, professionalism and passion for the development of the profession in view of his track record of excellence in the service of the Federal Radio Corporation of Nigeria for several years. I recall that Orji handled several sensitive assignments for the Corporation with distinction at those turbulent times in our Nation's history. For instance, as Radio Nigeria Correspondent attached to the President at the Presidential Villa, Aso Rock between 1992-2000, he left a very enduring legacy of professional excellence. He also shared this experience in his first book *Inside Aso Rock*. This book *What They Don't Teach You In Broadcasting* is the author's second book.

While reading through this comprehensive work, I was delighted to see that indeed major areas of information drought and practical challenges mostly experienced in the field by graduates of Mass Communication, working Journalists and the industry at large were sufficiently covered. These include the choice of the profession and how it works, working environment, practical issues involved in news development, presentation and production as well as what to expect when a reporter is assigned to cover an event but as a correspondent. Some interesting areas in the book which industry practitioners cannot ignore are; techniques in conducting interviews garnered from practical experience, coverage of major ceremonies of public interest, peculiarities in reporting for the broadcast media, the new media challenge, world information order, etc.

I am encouraged that a book relevant to education in the field of Mass Communication, which students, teachers and industry practitioners will find valuable has emerged from someone who is a product of our industry and our local environment.

I therefore wish to recommend this book to all media professionals and organisations, our universities, polytechnics, research institutions, schools and colleges, and the general public as a tool in bridging the gap between theory and practice.

Dr. Ladan Salihu
Director General
Federal Radio Corporation of Nigeria (FRCN)
Radio Nigeria Headquarters, Radio House
Abuja.
28th March, 2014.

Introduction

In the early days of my career as a broadcast journalist, people often asked me: "What do you see as the major driver of national development as our country steps into the 21st century?" I gave some serious thoughts to the question in those early days; is it our size, large population and market, our abundant human and natural resources, or our culture and good climate? But I did not make much progress.

At that time, Nigeria was under military dictatorship, with all kinds of draconian decrees defining rules of engagement with government, people, business and the environment. Yet, each time in the course of my sojourn in the media profession, the desire to provide precise and accurate answer to this fundamental question increased, not by relying on existing doctrines, but by allowing unfolding national and global developments set my mind and attention on possible answers.

Eventually the answer to the question began to evolve on their own after our nation successfully made a peaceful transition from military dictatorship to civilian rule on May 29th, 1999. It then became clearer to me that what should really be the major driver of national development in the new democratic Nigeria is the existence of a free, independent and responsible media, built strongly on the rule of law. Such media freedom would deepen and institutionalize our country's democratic values, culture and principles in both minds and attitudes of the people as fundamental conditions to promote good governance, transparency, accountability and rule of law.

At the heart of the media profession to carry out this function is the broadcasting industry; a section of the profession closer to the people at the grassroot, with the widest reach and convenience. The average Nigerian citizen is currently faced with basic challenges of poverty, unemployment, lack of basic healthcare, education and infrastructure.

It then became clear to me that for Nigeria to redefine its destiny, embrace and implement an appropriate development paradigm that will connect the average Nigerian with the government and its programmes, as well as connect the government with the peoples' needs and aspirations, exposure to information is key.

Access to information widens opportunities for citizens to make choices consistent with their needs and priorities. It narrows the gap between the poor and the rich, the weak and the strong. Availability of information equally helps in building confidence and trust between the government and the governed. It promotes civic education, citizens' participation, mobilization and development that shape the society.

Above all, with the availability of information, corruption is reduced, while an atmosphere for debates, discourses, discussions and advocacy for better governance is enhanced. This is why access to information and the rule of law remain the difference between developed, developing and under-developed countries.

It is within this context that the role of the media, especially radio and television in an underdeveloped nation like Nigeria, is located. But is the media and indeed, the broadcast media in its present form and structure, in any position to play these important roles effectively?

A close look at the content of Mass Communication courses available to students in most Nigerian Universities, Polytechnics and other institutions of higher learning, shows that the courses, with all good intentions and purposes, are designed to equip the students with requisite knowledge and skills to enable them respond adequately to the manpower needs of the media industry in Nigeria and beyond.

The expectation of these institutions is that Mass Communication graduates will adequately fit into the media industry with very little or no further training in the core areas of the profession. These are print, electronic, public relations, advertising, photography, information management, publishing, etc.

This expectation probably explains why the course contents and outlines in most of the institutions cover the basic and advanced areas such as introduction to Mass Communication, where the students are tutored on what the course is all about and what it is not; rudiments of reporting and news writing, and exposure to philosophy, psychology, sociology and allied disciplines to establish the strong connection between communication, society and human behaviour.

Students also go through lectures in broadcasting principles and practice, radio/TV production techniques, industry laws and ethics, public relations, advertising, newspaper production, arts and graphics development, precision reporting, critical writing, advanced composition, including research methods and photography, among others.

From more than three decades of practical experience in the industry which covers the major aspects of the media, especially as broadcast programs producer, presenter, reporter, correspondent, editor, news manager and as head of Media and Public Relations in several government agencies, experience has shown that there is a huge gap between what we learn in school and the practical industry experiences.

Some of the gaps are issues which cannot be easily envisaged by any school curriculum but constitute critical success factors in media practice in general, and broadcasting in particular. The huge gap has created a situation where most graduates in this discipline remain unemployed, under-employed or unemployable. It is also largely responsible for the falling standards of broadcasting in terms of content, quality, and ethics.

This Book, *What They Don't Teach You in Broadcasting,* is an experience-based knowledge sharing initiative with practical examples aimed at bridging the increasing gap between theory and practice. This book contains those issues, experiences and realities that we must encounter in the practice of the profession which we were not taught in school. It is a contribution to the efforts of our institutions and the media industry in building a functional bridge between the classroom and the field.

Written with electronic media background, *What They Don't Teach You in Broadcasting* is a good companion for all students of Mass Communication, media organizations, training institutions and practising journalists, set to face realities as well as challenges in the media profession.

Orji Ogbonnaya Orji, *PhD*
Maitama, Abuja, Nigeria
January 25th, 2014.

Chapter 1

Journey into Broadcasting

Everyone has a story. And this book is part of my own story. My journey into broadcasting was neither a design nor a plan. And most broadcasters I know share similar stories and circumstances. In most cases, the journey into broadcasting was accidental. I am yet to come across anyone who planned or designed the choice except Bisi Olatilo, a former colleague in Radio Nigeria Lagos.

Narrating how he joined broadcasting in an interview with Punch Newspapers of February 1, 2014, Bisi recalled:

> *"I had no other life ambition even from my secondary school days. Those days, we used to have small televisions. I would always listen to the News at 7 am, 4 pm and 10 pm and the words I heard would keep resonating. The voice of Ikenna Ndaguba was always reading the Network News then. For Football, it was Ishola*

Folorunsho. They were the ones reigning then. By the time I was in school, I got fascinated and I started doing things like that. During my school days, my Principal then, Mr Olagunju allowed me and gave me the latitude to gather news around our environment, prepare it and read to the Assembly of not less than one thousand people and they will all listen to me. We also had football matches and did mock football commentaries at that young age. And so the breakthrough came. After my school, I approached the Broadcasting Corporation of Oyo State. That was the Radio Station where I started before I came over to Lagos and the coast became a lot wider."

Bisi Olatilo grew in broadcasting to become a renowned presenter, network newscaster and General Manager of Radio Nigeria 3, FM (national languages) station Lagos, before a glorious exit to the private sector where he is currently the Chief Executive of Biscom Communications group. His organization anchors the *Bisi Olatilo Show* on national television networks. His kind of story is peculiar, unique and few.

In my own case, the sojourn into broadcasting was largely by accident. Fresh from Saint John Bosco Secondary School, now Ishiagu High School in the then Okigwe province in 1980, the future appeared quite bright for many in my set who looked forward to getting a job and building a career in the civil service. At that time, with a good grade in the West African School Certificate, a job in the civil service, especially teaching, was guaranteed.

2

And so, with that limited exposure, there was little or no information available about options of other professions, including broadcasting, apart from the civil service, especially for young school leavers. If anything, we were among the category of children who wondered if those voices we heard daily on radio actually belonged to human beings.

In developing countries and among rural dwellers in those days, radio was simply "a scientific and technological discovery which only the white man was in a position to explain." In my village, as in any other at the time, it was a mystery to many how a human being could squeeze himself into the radio (which existed in various sizes), speak to listeners in an original voice and the message is received loud and clear, far and wide, in a manner that inspires and influences both human behavior and activities.

Radio, as a means of communication therefore, was a mystery and what an Igbo man would call *"Bekee wu agbara"*, meaning the white man is a deity; an oracle. And if radio was a mystery, how does one explain the similar science and technology behind the television which combines audio and visual capabilities in information dissemination, educating and entertaining the audience. I was among the teaming Nigerian children born and raised in the rural areas that grew up with this broadcasting myth.

On 18th January 1981, the then Imo State Broadcasting Service (IBS) Owerri, one of the new but very popular radio stations on the east of the Niger, announced through its regular news and programmes that all graduates of

Secondary Schools with good grades in West African School Certificate should report at the Imo State Civil Service Commission for possible recruitment into the State Civil Service. My visit to Owerri was in response to this public service announcement over the IBS.

But on arrival at the Commission Headquarters in Owerri, then located at Okigwe Road, we were informed that the exercise had been shifted to a later date. The Chairman of the Imo State Civil Service Commission at the time, Dr Agom Eze, conveyed the message to the young school leavers who had promptly responded to the invitation. Dr Agom Eze, with regrets and apologies, directed that names of all those who honored the invitation, especially from outside Owerri, be compiled instantly for compensation with some stipend to enable them return to their various destinations with minimal pain, pending when the exercise will take place. At that time, job seekers and applicants in Nigeria were treated with some dignity, respect and courtesy.

The stipend so provided turned out to be a windfall; more than enough for a poor job seeker, that I decided to change destination and headed to Enugu. And my mission in Enugu was to try my luck in another job opportunity which I learnt existed at the Nigerian Railway Corporation at the time.

The Railway corporation, a functional, effective and big employer of labour in Nigeria at that time, was recruiting young officers to fill vacancies that existed in its Eastern District offices. The trip from Owerri to Enugu

4

was by a local bus. On arrival in Garki, Awkunanaw, Enugu Motor Park, the bus conductor who was quite rude paired me with one other passenger to sort ourselves out over change issues, claiming he had no change for either of us. Before we could make any form of protest as we did not know each other, the conductor jumped into his moving vehicle and began yelling for new passengers.

We looked at each other with initial anger and surprise, had no other option than to grab our destiny in our hands, and began a search for change to sort out ourselves. In the process, we made some introductions, during which my enforced partner introduced himself as a staff of Radio Nigeria. That changed my mood as I proceeded to bombard him with all the questions and answers I had harboured from my rural background about the mystery of the radio. I immediately requested to visit him for purposes of sightseeing and excursions and nothing else. My new friend readily obliged. That was the first step of my journey into broadcasting.

I visited the Radio Nigeria Broadcasting House, located at Onitsha Road, Enugu, courtesy of my new friend. He took time off his job to take me round the studios and offices. I was amazed at the environment which was created by the serenity, orderliness, discipline, comportment and simplicity of all the staff that I met. Everyone I met was warm, pleasant, and friendly. The broadcasting house was neat, relaxed and a reflection of an environment where knowledge, freedom and entertainment flowed freely.

The staff members were eager to explain their work, the broadcasting value chain, how the message originates from the studios, through the announcer/presenter, to the control room via the transmitting station through the frequencies and how the signals are received on air on our radio sets and to the listener. My host ensured that I watched live broadcast of news and programmes, allowed me access to interact with announcers and presenters whose voices I was familiar with on radio over the years.

It was such a major exposure and experience of a lifetime. The visit freed me from my village myth of the radio. While thanking my host for such rare opportunity, I curiously inquired, "What does it take to work here?" My host replied, "To be a broadcaster, you must be naturally endowed with creativity, innovation and a good voice. A broadcaster needs at least basic knowledge and interest in everything - business, economy, public policies, contemporary issues, current affairs, politics, sports, education, health, science, religion, culture, the good, the bad and the ugly and most importantly, how issues about them shape people and events in our environment."

"My friend," he added as a note of warning, "a broadcaster must be ready to be jack of all trades and master of all. Ignorance has no place in a broadcasting house because the profession is knowledge-driven. Besides, you must be ready to move against the traffic in your ideas, logic and reasoning," he concluded. "How does one move against the traffic?" I curiously queried. My friend stared at me in a manner that suggested that I was indeed inexperienced.

In apparent realization that I needed more information, my host handed me an application form and some publications which essentially contained basic public education materials including news and programmes schedule of Radio Nigeria, Enugu. The publications were freely displayed at the public reception areas at the entrance of the Broadcasting House. When I got home, I took time to study the application form and read through the publications as I began to imagine a possible career in broadcasting amidst other possible job opportunities.

I completed the application form the next day and headed to the broadcasting house to submit same to the Zonal Director as boldly instructed on the form. Unknown to me, issuance and return of application forms was an assignment for an ordinary clerk in the organisation's general office. There was no reason whatsoever to take such a pedestrian matter to the big man, a whole Zonal Director, who at the time was in charge of all the States in the present day South-East, South-South zones as well as some parts of the Middle Belt, including Benue State. I do not know till today how I got straight to the Zonal Director without any of his numerous aides at the check-points stopping me. His secretary and aides who indeed could have stopped me were not on seat, thus giving me direct access to his office.

A knock at the door and a polished, pleasant voice asked me to come in. The door opened and I was face to face with a man whom many staff in the organization may not have had reasons to visit in all their career. I stared at the opulent, magnificent and well-furnished office. Until that encounter, the best office I had entered before was

7

that of my school principal.

As I savored the ambience of my new environment, the Zonal Director offered me a sit and humbled me with an introduction, "Young man, my name is Ralph Opara, what can I do for you?" I muttered in a trembling low voice, "Good morning sir, I need a job?" He looked at me and repeated, "You need a job?" "Yes sir," I answered and quickly opened a worn-out file jacket and handed over my completed application form with the attached WASC Result and School Leaving Testimonial.

The Director put on his reading glasses, glanced through my documents and surprisingly, the Zonal Director was attracted by my handwriting and immediately inquired if the writing was indeed mine. I said it was. "Your hand-writing is nice," he commended. "Thank you very much Sir," I replied. He took a golden pen, wrote something on the application, pressed his bell and a lady entered. He asked me to follow the lady whom I then understood was his secretary. The lady told me to go, that I will hear from them. I did. One week later, I was invited for an interview and offered a job as a Clerical Officer at the Federal Radio Corporation of Nigeria, FRCN Enugu.

However, on resumption, I soon discovered that my job schedule as a clerk only saddled me with administrative duties. I had no doubt made some progress in the journey but I was far from broadcasting. I then began to plot and consult widely for a possible inter-departmental transfer to News and Programmes Department, the professional peak of the job.

To achieve the transfer, I was advised that one easy way was for me to demonstrate exceptional interest and skills in various programmes and news activities of the station so as to merit a possible move. To this end, I requested for an audition, a mandatory exercise required to ascertain my voice quality and suitability among other things.

After a successful audition, I was then assigned an early morning soul-lifting religious programme in Igbo, called *egwu eji etochineke* meaning, 'music to praise God'. The big question was how do I proceed on the programme when I hardly speak Igbo fluently without interjecting with English? In my secondary school, I did more of science and arts subjects and never offered Igbo as a subject. I did very well in all science subjects including Chemistry. How then do I blend into my new role as presenter of an Igbo programme to a predominantly Igbo audience which Enugu and the South-East represent? That was a challenge.

Nonetheless, I was determined to fit into the role, after all, Igbo was supposed to be my mother-tongue and first language and some of my friends had told me that broadcasting requires moving against the traffic, that it is about potential and possibilities, not limits. At this point, the 'I can do it spirit' took over.

The programme, *egwu eji eto chineke* was on air every Sunday Morning from 6. 15 am to 8 am in the then Medium Wave Service of Radio Nigeria, Enugu. I anchored the programme with my all. Thus, the programme became so popular that listeners across the zone often looked forward to it before proceeding to church on Sundays. The programme became so successful that I became a regularly invited guest at most major Christian gatherings and church programmes.

Over time, bishops and church leaders in Enugu and environs found it expedient to consult me on religious issues. The programme *egwu eji etochineke* imposed on me an image and a reputation that was very different from my original personality. Unknown to my admirers on the programme at the time, I hardly go to church on my own or got committed to any church activity. At that time, I was not a bad boy, just an Enugu boy, freely enjoying myself, available for all forms of social gatherings and parties in town. But I was careful and conscious of the job I did and the false image it had given me before my listeners.

The professional and public exposure I got from that programme defined the power and influence of radio clearly; that in broadcasting, a presenter can be in 'borrowed robes', unknown to the audience and admirers.

From that experience, I learnt that before a presenter goes on air to speak to the public, he/she must be armed with a script on what to say. The script must be developed by the presenter in line with the programme content and outline. It must be duly vetted by the producer of the programme. I also learnt that it was ethically a taboo and aberration in broadcasting to jump into the studio to present a live programme without a script. At that time, the punishment was better imagined than described.

For a music programme, developing a script is easier as it is aided by the music compilation. The presenter must create time to prepare for the programme. The venue for such preparation is the library within the broadcasting house which is fully equipped with all kinds of music, both ancient and modern. Also in the library are usually recorded tapes of previously produced programmes which the presenter is free to explore as reference material.

The librarians in the broadcasting house are trained to guide users on any information that they may require. In short, in the library, all material required to support a presenter to prepare for a programme are easily made available. As part of the preparations, the presenter must make a decision on the type and nature of music to be used for the programme, the duration, alignment and sequence. The bottom line is that mistakes are forbidden.

Sunday July 4, 1982 is a day I will always remember. It was the day I said my first word and made my first presentation on radio. I recorded that date in my diary. The preparations for that day were as comprehensive and sensitive to me as the apprehension. I had informed friends and family members from far and near to tune to the station and listen to me as a new anchor of a new programme. The invitations were received with high expectations and attended admiration.

Friends and family members whose radio sets had one form of problems or the other had hurriedly repaired them while others had to procure batteries to avoid likely disappointment by NEPA. I therefore went to bed the previous night with high hopes that all was set to launch the journey into broadcasting. I hardly closed my eyes throughout the night for fear of missing the driver on early shift designated to pick me to the station.

Because the station opens at 5.30 a.m each day, all those whose programmes and work schedule fall within the morning shift must be picked up from their various homes to the station on or before 5 a.m unfailingly. In broadcasting, there is no African time. Punctuality is indeed the soul of the business. The moment finally arrived, the announcer on duty after the early morning news summary launched the programme and ushered me live on air. I quickly played the signature tune designed to alert listeners that the programme had started. As the music was playing, I looked up and saw that all staff on duty had gathered at the other end of the studio to watch how I would perform. That alone added to the tension, fear and pressure that suddenly enveloped me. As the cue light came on, I opened my mouth to greet and share pleasantries with the listeners, I was surprised as I listened to myself through the ear phone that my voice remained original, that I sounded natural, real and normal. This gave me added confidence as I battled to overcome every other fear. My confidence increased as the programme progressed and I began to enjoy myself.

At the end of the programme, comments, criticisms and commendations from the producer, members of staff, family members, friends and listeners began to pour in. The comments from those who should know were encouraging. The keep- it- ups were more. Of interest was that no one criticized my Igbo because I chose to speak the Igbo I know in my natural format. And so I gained confidence and looked forward to the second edition of the programme with renewed zeal, interest and optimism.

Egwu eji eto chineke, the first live programme I ever produced and presented on radio exposed me to basic rudiments of presentation; the procedure and discipline required to anchor weekly live programmes, the commitment to keep a date with the listener by making sure that the programme comes up on schedule every week, challenges of studio phobia, audience reactions and many more that helped to shape my career in those early inquisitive days and years that followed. It was an experience that defined a long journey.

Chapter 2

The Broadcasting Environment

The broadcasting house largely defines the broadcasting environment in more ways than one. It is a market environment for information, education entertainment, and above all, ideas. The environment can be fun for those who work in it during and after work hours.

The broadcasting environment contains the studios, the control rooms, the library and other major installations. The studios include live studios for programmes and news presentations, talk studios for interviews and recording studios for programmes and news productions.

In some cases, especially in the emerging digital broadcasting, the transmitters are equally housed in the broadcasting house. Also in the broadcasting house are offices of core professional departments such as the various units of the News and Programmes divisions. These include the newsrooms, news and programmes production offices, editorial meeting and conference rooms, maintenance offices and allied services considered quite essential for quick interventions in news and programmes operations.

Other departments that provide support services are usually housed outside of the broadcasting house. But all the buildings and offices and the staff who work in them constitute, in this context, the broadcasting environment.

The culture that regulates the conduct of staff in the broadcasting house is quite different. Inside the broadcasting house, conduct of staff is largely regulated in a manner similar to that of the church or in a hospital ward in terms of decorum. Noise making, loitering and any other form of distraction is prohibited.

The staff who work in the broadcasting house are usually trained to internalize the ambience of the broadcasting environment. There are usually signals and cue lights to draw staff and visitors' attention to the fact that they are within a broadcasting house and around studio areas. Comportment, decorum and serenity are essential ethical standards of behaviour upheld within the broadcasting house and environment.

This notwithstanding, the environment, more often than not, is fun, especially during music programmes. The staff who work in this environment are themselves sources of happiness to the society and share same among one another. This they do while still abiding to the culture of the environment which they have come to internalize as a way of life while on duty. The FRCN broadcasting houses nationwide, especially at the national and zonal headquarters in Abuja, Lagos, Ibadan, Kaduna and Enugu reflect this ambience.

On my various visits to BBC Bush House London, Voice of America and the Radio Deutsche Welle in Bonn Germany, I found it amazing that the structure of the broadcasting environment in these world class stations were largely the same with the ones in Nigeria. However, the equipment and digital installations, as well as the maintenance culture, are in no way comparable with ours.

Apart from behavioural ethics, the broadcasting environment worldwide is known to generally promote entertainment, learning and information. The news rooms, the studios and the offices are centers of debates, arguments and discussions over the merits or demerits of contemporary issues of public policy, policy options, governance, human and capacity utilization, among others. This is common in the news rooms during production hours and in the studios when there are no ongoing live programmes.

A studio is described as live when the programmes and news being transmitted from that studio is not recorded. These include news on the hour such as the 7 am, 4pm and 10 pm major news bulletin broadcasts on the network service of Radio Nigeria, for instance. Other live programmes include listeners request programmes on radio, and telephone chit chat interactive programmes. A studio therefore becomes live if the output from the studio is fresh, current and not recorded. A live studio is created based on the need.

In the broadcast environment, debates over phonetics, pronunciation of names of news makers, towns and villages and appropriate meanings or synonyms of key English or vernacular words are common. The challenging names cut across and reflect the diversity of Nigeria - Ibo, Yoruba, Hausa/Fulani, etc. But specially challenging are names from some parts of Tiv tribe of Benue, Izon in Bayelsa, Bini names in Edo State and names from Plateau State, especially if the newscasters or presenters come from outside these areas.

News, Presentation and Program Operations

In many ways, the convergence of news, programme presentations and programmes operations represents the mirror with which the broadcasting house can be seen and measured. These key operational areas drive the content, quality and direction of the organization if it is built solidly on sound engineering base. Let us now examine specifically what each of these key elements in broadcasting add to the broadcasting value chain and the broadcasting environment.

News Department

Because the entire concept of the media, whether print or electronic, is anchored on the principle of information, the News Department is the principal pillar of broadcasting. It can therefore be called *Primus inter Pares* - the first among equals. Among other key tasks, the News Department is responsible for content development, sourcing, management and implementation of news and editorial policies of the broadcasting organization. The department also advises the management on news and information policy direction of the station in line with the vision and mission of the organization. The News department is usually divided into units for purposes of division of labour. The department is usually headed by a professional journalist with solid news background, industry exposure and knowledge of public policy. The units are under the supervision of Sectional Heads. The department is a major operational area in a broadcasting environment.

The Reporters Corps

The Reporters Corps or Unit is headed by a Manager or Controller who reports directly to the Director of News. The Corps or Unit, as the case may be, is primarily responsible for sourcing stories from the fields of assignment. It is an important part of the broadcast environment. The Reporters Corps also has the duty of feeding the newsroom regularly with current and reliable stories from the field on daily and timely basis. The fields of assignments include designated beats such as the legislature, judiciary, State house, business and finance, politics, health, education, etc. Some of the beats have regular correspondents attached to them.

The Reporters Corps has the responsibility of maintaining a register of all invitations for news coverage extended to the station. In addition, this unit coordinates and manages reporters and correspondents to ensure prompt attendance and response to invitations and assignments. It is also the duty of the Reporters Corps to bring to the attention of the News Department any event or public policy that requires media coverage.

In the same vein, such duties as commissioning special reports on key public policies and contemporary issues fall within the role of the unit. The Reporters Corps also takes interest in carrying out special investigations on matters of public interest and provides balanced account for the public to judge. It advises the News Department on matters related to origin, importance, risks and benefits of news reports, among others.

The Network News Reporters Corps at the Broadcasting House Ikoyi, Lagos during my time was fun. We were a wonderful professional family. Tajudeen Akanbi was the Head of the Corps. Looking back, I remember great reporters like Tony Akiotu who was the head of our Sports Desk. Tony was an authority in sports reporting and a resource person in sports administration in Nigeria at the time. His reports on the Network News set agenda for sports fans and enthusiasts. Tony Akiotu is currently the Group Managing Director of Daar Communications, the owners of African Independent Television and Ray Power radio networks. Then there was Reginald Okochi who was our State House Correspondent at the Dodan Barracks. ROK, as we fondly call him, was a fine reporter with a commanding personality. Many of us respected and looked up to him. I later worked under him at the Dodan Barracks, Lagos, and took over from him at the Presidential Villa, Abuja, as Radio Nigeria Chief State House Correspondent.

His track record put me on edge and geared me to learn the ropes quickly. We also had in the Corps, Joseph Azoro, on the Diplomatic beat. Judicial correspondent, Kelly Elisha used to break down issues in court proceedings, interpret landmark judgments, rulings and litigations to minute details for the grassroot audience.

Gbenga Onayiga was also a part of the family. So also was Pius Ebohon and Emma Enwose, both of blessed memory. In the Reporters Corps, we competed favourably in a friendly and cordial manner in the areas of competence, networking, knowledge sharing, relevance and dependability. When all reports have gone and production time is over, we relaxed in the Reporters Corps to crack very expensive jokes over our problems, failures and conditions of service. The jokes were in no small measures efforts to reduce pressure and cushion the effects of the hardship created by the work environment. It was a job we loved even in the midst of those conditions.

The jokes in the Reporters Corps often attracted our bosses who found the laughter and humour irresistible. For instance, our late colleague, Pius Ebohon, was well-known to start the jokes all the time. Pius would move from desk to desk to ask if anyone needed financial help, claiming that he had more than enough to lend, provided that his 'victim' was prepared to bring both parents as a guarantor. His argument was that "for your parents you left behind in the village to travel to Lagos to come and bail you out, will leave no one, including your parents, in doubt that you have failed." As a result of the humourous and conducive atmosphere in the Reporters Corps and the news room after production hour and the notorious Lagos Traffic on the

Third Mainland and Carter Bridges, many of us preferred to wait for the traffic to ease and enjoy more jokes as part of dividend of the broadcast environment.

This same Pius, of blessed memory, would move from one person to the other, asking if anyone had problems with his or her landlord. It was very common for tenants in Lagos who were indebted to their landlords to sneak into their apartments when the landlord must have gone to bed and sneak out very early in the morning before the landlord wakes up. Pius claimed he had the capacity to intervene and publicly invited whoever refused to go home to embrace his offers. The jokes also covered grammatical mistakes and mispronounciation of any word or name on air. This team spirit served as peer review and positive checks and balances in the approach to our duties both at the broadcasting house and within the broadcasting environment.

Editorial Unit

In the broadcasting environment, the duty of the editorial unit is to coordinate and manage the news room during and after production time. The production time is the period that the unit is receiving and collating stories to produce a bulletin to be broadcast at a specific news time belt. The production time is usually a very busy time within which no other thing matters except to the get the bulletin ready. The editor on shift is the alpha and omega during the shift. He has the power to reject or throw away any story he considers not good enough.

The job of the editorial unit is therefore to collect, collate, rewrite and mould a story submitted by the reporter into a news item. The editorial unit edits, and ensures that all stories are proofread and error free. They edit the stories for error, size, content, comprehension, context and meaning. They also check the stories for balance, objectivity, sensitivity, fairness, truth and reliability. The editor uses the house style of the station as a guide. Any sloppiness in casting, grammar or style will be the burden of the editor and his editorial department, and they will answer for it at the subsequent editorial meeting. The weekly or daily editorial meeting was a review and agenda-setting forum, where everyone learns from each other's accomplishments and mistakes.

The editorial unit represents the engine room of news production. This is why it is usually staffed with knowledgeable, diligent, and patient officers with eyes for details. The editorial unit is further divided into shifts to ensure sustained and continuous news production. It is the duty of the unit to align stories in order of importance. The editor also decides which story makes a headline.

I spent a good period of my career in the news department. I had the opportunity to work in the editorial unit under several editors, some of whom I can hardly forget. Two of my favorites were Victor Kodeso and Tayo Takuro. Victor Kodeso (now Oviedje Kodeso on the AIT/ Raypower group) was one editor whose bulletin made every story look important no matter how watery the contents may be. He had a rare gift of adding strength to a story without changing the facts. Besides, his use of the English language was superb and flawless. When he picked and cast headlines, one could not but admire his sense of news judgment.

Tayo Takuro also shared these attributes with Victor. It was pretty tough working with them. I do not know where Tayo is now, but I learnt quite a lot, working with them in the editorial unit at the Broadcasting House, Ikoyi Lagos. Another younger and good editor I noticed each time I listened to my reports or went into the newsroom during his shift was Haruna Idris. Haruna had the comportment and eye for details. He could look at stories scattered before him and tell at a glance if the shift had enough lines of stories to make a good bulletin.

Current Affairs Unit

This unit, which can be headed by a Manager or Controller, coordinates and manages all current affairs issues for the attention of the News Department within and outside the broadcast environment. Current affairs issues in broadcasting include, but are not limited to, matters of the moment, either recent or unfolding, currently in the public domain and provoking public discourse, debate, agitation, protests and discussions. These may have arisen from a new or existing public policy, government pronouncements, natural disaster, labour unrest, acts of aggression or oppression, etc.

For example, at the time of writing this page, the current affairs issues in Nigeria include the removal of Mallam Sanusi Lamido Sanusi as Central Bank Governor, the mass killings of about 59 students of a Federal Government College in Yobe State by the Boko Haram insurgence in North Eastern Nigeria, the political crisis in Rivers State, Nigeria's Centenary Celebration, among others.

The work of the unit is to deepen rational and constructive public understanding, provide balanced information through promotion of social commentary, public opinions, discussions and debates around these issues in news and current affairs programmes. The unit therefore deliberately creates news programmes, editorials, news analysis and commentary to advance the discourses.

Examples of current affairs programmes on Radio Nigeria are the following: Radio Link on Radio Nigeria; a popular audience participation programme, Political Platform of the AIT/Ray Power, Eagles Square of Radio Nigeria (FRCN) and the Sunrise Daily on Channels TV, etc. Others include daily news commentary and analysis on key national issues and developments. The current affairs unit also provides research services to the news department.

Programmes Department

The programmes department, like the news department, is headed by a Director, with a number of Managers and Controllers in charge of the various units and departments of programmes. Although news is, technically speaking, a programme, the programme department is responsible for all non-news output of the organisation, such as Drama, Features and Documentaries, etc. The department is also responsible for content development, sourcing, management and implementation of programme policies of the broadcasting organization. The department also advises the Station on programmes development, dissemination and benefits with the specific goal of creating desired national and international attention and awareness on areas of national priorities. These include health, education, infrastructure, poverty, anti-corruption and other governance challenges. For instance, on public health, the programmes department can develop programmes to create awareness and debates on health hazards or a national epidemic like malaria spread, guinea worm, cholera, HIV AIDS, cancer and hypertension.

On education, the department can develop similar campaigns to draw attention to issues like poor quality of primary education and the dangers to national development, discrimination against girl-child education, poor school enrolment in sections of the country, cultism in schools, and poor learning environment in schools and colleges. On governance, the department is responsible for creating awareness through programmes on issues like dangers of corruption, poor voters' education, public sector reforms, etc. The department also advises the station on the programme policies of the Station, in line with the vision and mission of the organization.

The programme department is equally divided into units for purposes of division of labour. The units are under the supervision of sectional heads who may be called Principals or Managers.

Expectedly, the department is headed by a professional with sound background in programmes and presentation techniques, industry exposure and knowledge of public policy.

The Production Unit

This unit is primarily responsible for sourcing ideas and programme concepts. The unit is usually staffed with trained producers, who develop these ideas and concepts into programme topics. The people in this unit are responsible for developing a story line based on history and present realities and moulding them into a programme format with an objective, duration, desired impact, benefits and target audience in mind. Producing a programme requires deep thinking which comes from a knowledgeable, innovative and creative mind. A good producer grabs the attention of the listener, takes over his mind and makes him ponder a situation while proffering possible solutions to the issues at hand.

To achieve this feat, the producer requires a good knowledge of the material to use, the resource persons required to participate in the programme, where to find both the resource persons and the material and the capacity to comprehensively package the programme. A good and well-produced programme, in my view, requires, but is not limited, to the following:

- A good producer
- A good idea developed with good concepts
- A good script
- A trained voice to handle the narration
- Intelligent resource persons
- Good studio effects
- Good studio hands
- Good editing and *post mortem*
- Good timing and duration e.g. a 30 minutes programme should not exceed 28 minutes.

The production unit, through the continuity studio, feeds the station regularly with programmes on various issues for broadcasts at designated time schedules during daily transmission.

Presentation Unit

The presentation unit is staffed with presenters and announcers whose job is to run the continuity studios of the station round the clock on shift time basis. The announcers and presenters are primarily employed for possessing audible and pleasant voices so as to anchor the news and programmes of the station.

The announcers on duty manage the programmes and news schedule of the broadcasting house. The continuity announcer is on duty from the time the station opens in the morning until close down at midnight. But for stations running a 24-hour service as it is the case now in modern broadcasting, the announcers are on duty all the time. During every shift, the duty continuity announcer is in charge. The announcer uses the running order as a guide. The running order contains a schedule of all programmes and advertisements slated to be aired on the station throughout the day's broadcast.

The announcer is to follow the running order diligently and ensure its strict compliance by all who work in the studio during the shift. With the running order, the Announcer is clear about the specific time one programme ends and when another begins. The announcer is equally aware of how many advertisements are scheduled for broadcast, where the recorded materials are kept and the officers responsible for them. The announcer uses his/her golden voice to launch those programs or advertisements at the beginning or sign them off at the end.

This is why any careful announcer on resumption of duty, uses the running order to check the location and identity of any programme slated for broadcast. Any programme scheduled in the running order that goes wrong under the watch of any announcer is a serious offence in broadcasting. The programmes under the supervision of the announcer include live and recorded programmes. Live programmes include news on the hour, music and chit-chat programmes and listeners request. Each live programme has a scheduled presenter. The presenter comes in on schedule and is launched on air to present the programme. At the end of the duration of the programme, the presenter signs off while the announcer continues by wrapping up the programme and introducing another one. The announcer is therefore an indispensable link during live transmissions.

The job of an announcer is similar to that of a Master of Ceremony in an event. One important duty of the announcer, often ignored in today's broadcasting, is ensuring that all presenters who come into a Live Studio to present any programme are armed with a vetted script for the programme. The script must be shown and sighted before the announcer is obliged to launch such a presenter.

Unfortunately, however, what we find today is that presenters jump into the studio with no script or any form of preparation. The wrong usage of the English language, and infantile approach to presentation that is prevalent has affected the quality of broadcasts and are largely responsible for dwindling listeners' confidence. The announcer is under the supervision of the Head of Presentation. The presentation unit also provides newscasters with trained voices that read the news on the hour.

The Library, Research and Documentation Unit

The Library is the knowledge reservoir and archival base in the broadcasting house. A broadcasting house without a library is like a bank without a safe. The library keeps in safe custody all news and programmes broadcast of a station in stored, recorded and archived format for reference purposes. Such stored and secured programmes and news become very useful for purposes of conflict prevention, management and resolution.

The second function of the library is to house all recorded daily or weekly programmes until they are set for broadcast at designated periods. Thus, each programme has a secured place in the library where they are carefully kept. The library also serves as a safe haven for programmes that might require repeat broadcast. The producer in charge keeps such programmes until they are scheduled for broadcast.

The library is also the place where all records and music are stored in their various grades and categories. These include jazz, highlife, pop, religious, classical, blues, etc. In the music section in the library, the broadcaster is exposed to all kinds of music sufficient to meet specific audience and programme needs.

The library also provides a very serene environment for reading, research, reviews, script development, writing and editing required by a broadcaster to prepare adequately for a programme or news presentation. In the library, all major national and international speeches made since Nigeria's independence can be found. These include independence day broadcasts by former and present Nigerian leaders, budget broadcasts, state of the nation addresses and the speeches made on behalf of the nation at international fora such as the United Nations.

Many of us were either too young or not born when Tafawa Balewa was Prime Minister of Nigeria and may not know that he was perhaps the most eloquent speaker of the English language Nigeria ever produced at that level. His nickname was 'The Golden Voice'. I was amazed when I ran into one of the national speeches he made to the nation at Nigeria's Independence celebration and another he delivered in the chambers of the United Nations General Assembly. I stumbled on the recorded tapes at the Radio Nigeria headquarters library while preparing for a news programme. The library is usually managed by competent librarians who know where to find what, even at short notice.

Engineering Department

The Engineering Department is the bone and the central nervous system in broadcasting. Until it was restructured during the tenure of Eddie Iroh, as Director-General of FRCN (1999-2005), it was called Technical Services Department. Engineering as a support service is key to news and program operations in the broadcasting environment. The department is responsible for providing all technical dynamics required for a programme and news signal to move from the studio through the audio mixer console to the control, passing through the transmitting station to the air waves where the signals are then instantly received with the speed of light, through our radio sets.

The work of engineering in the broadcasting chain is likened to what the average Igbo man will consider and conclude as *"bekee wu agbara"* meaning the white man is simply a spirit, an oracle, or a deity. The department functions in various units and sections to get the job done. These include the transmitting station, the control room, operational repairs and maintenance and outside broadcast units.

In professional broadcasting, a sound, reliable and well-equipped engineering base is important. In the broadcasting house, News, Programmes and Engineering constitute the three most important departments. These departments remain the professional tripod on which the broadcasting house stands. This is in consideration of the fact that in any broadcasting organization, the quality of its news and programmes content and the clarity and reach of its signals define the character as well as the reputation of the station in the broadcast industry.

The importance of each of these units used to be the crux of arguments in the early days of my career in Enugu. At that time, I was in the programmes division. One fateful day, I was on air presenting a live programme. Unknown to me, the transmitting signal and the control had gone off, and the engineering staff on duty ignored me as they battled to restore transmission. When transmission was eventually restored, they came into the studio and informed me that for the last 15 minutes I had been talking to myself; that the transmitters and control room facilities and equipment were off. "Please play music or the station's ID now to enable the re-establishment of signals. And when we give you hand signals, please apologize to listeners for that break in transmission, give a time check and continue with the programme," they commanded. I obeyed the instruction with all humility. Since that day, I have appreciated the importance of the engineering department in the broadcasting value chain.

However, when I moved to the news department, the debate became even more interesting, this time creating rivalry and discrimination between each department with each one exploring every opportunity to assert its importance. The debate is still on-going but the reality is that all departments – News, Programmes, Engineering, Marketing, etc., are all critical to the success of broadcasting. But this ought not to be an issue for me, as my on-air experience proved. Even more clearly was the viewpoint that Eddie Iroh stressed often during his time as Director-General. It was his firm belief that, within the tripod of departments that held up the organisation, "Radio Nigeria will be only as strong as its weakest link." In other words, for any broadcasting organisation to function effectively, all departments need each other to achieve the set goals of serving the nation.

I started my career in the administration department from where I was transferred to programmes and later moved to the news department. I am therefore in a position to appreciate the fact that the work of all the departments are critical success factors in the broadcasting house and environment if the goal of the station as platform for public education, enlightenment, information and entertainment is to be met. However, News, Programmes and Engineering are the three main professional nerve of the broadcasting house in any broadcasting environment.

Administration and Finance Department

The administration department has the responsibility of providing administrative and support services to a broadcasting organization. It manages the broadcasting environment. The department is expected to handle and manage such issues as staff recruitment, appointments, promotion and discipline. It is also responsible for managing staff welfare, human resources issues, personnel emoluments, training and manpower development, logistics and allied matters. The department is further divided into administration and finance, training, etc. The structures of different broadcast organizations vary.

In my view, and from industry experience, the administration and finance department is in no position to make good judgments over the professional departments in a good broadcasting organization as it is common in many broadcasting houses, especially in the public sector environment in Nigeria.

In Bristol, England, where I had my advanced course as an internship while on a Commonwealth Fellowship in the United Kingdom in 1995, it was interesting to find how the station functioned effectively with little or no administrative bottlenecks. This is one area where reforms in public sector should face. It is necessary to put the professional departments in a position where their functions, which is of primary interest to the investors in the industry and the listeners, is carried out freely and with fewer bottlenecks.

35

Marketing Department

In the emerging and unavoidable regime of deregulation and privatization of the public-owned broadcast media, the role of the marketing department becomes easier to appreciate. The responsibility of the department is higher at a time like this when government subventions and budgetary provisions are steadily on the decline. Most of the broadcasting organizations therefore are left with the choice of sourcing funds through aggressive marketing.

For the private-owned broadcasting organisations, internally generated revenues through marketing are sure ways of survival in an industry that has become very competitive. The marketing department is therefore responsible for the following, among others:

- Sourcing advertisement for the station's news and programmes.
- Generating revenues internally to compliment other revenue sources.
- Developing ideas that will help market the Station's news and programmes.
- Advising the broadcast organization on viable options of funding.
- Building client's confidence and interest in the ability of the station's news and programme content to meet their peculiar advertisement needs.

In the pursuit of these and more marketing functions, many broadcast stations appear to jeopardize their editorial/professional reputation, organizational identity, independence, public interest and industry esteem. This is dangerous to the broadcasting industry.

As an organization, there must have been some passion, mission, vision and certain core values which the organization was set up to pursue and achieve. While appreciating the need to improve revenue generation to sustain operations, it is very important that the core values of the station, the mission and vision are not sacrificed on the altar of marketing. In Radio Nigera, the mission, vision, and indeed our passion were redefined and reaffirmed from 1999, under a democratic government. The reforms which I propose, is to return all public-owned media organisations to the original owners, the people, not just the government.This will help to change the citizens' perception that public funded radio stations are simply government 'praise singers.'

Chapter 3

The Broadcaster and the Society

The broadcaster, for purposes of our discourse, is one involved in education, entertainment and dissemination of information, through audio-visual means, using electromagnetic radiation through either radio or television, or both. This definition is by no means exhaustive but it does attempt to capture the statutory role of a broadcaster in the mass media chain.

They are some other roles that the society has imposed on the broadcaster by virtue of the nature of his assigned duties. But far more important is the nature of these roles, how the broadcast operators understand them and the attendant public perception and pressure which the broadcaster has to contend with in the discharge of these functions.

These and many more make the job of a broadcaster not just interesting, prestigious and noble, but one that puts the broadcaster under endless pressure. For the society, the broadcaster is knowledgeable and is a jack of all trades and master of all. Again, the broadcaster is perceived as a role model, one who understands the people better, preaches against oppression, injustice, corruption and poor governance.

The broadcaster is expected to be in the vanguard in the fight against poverty, social and political deprivation, unemployment, ignorance and disease. The broadcaster is also expected to use his medium to push down all boundaries of hatred, discrimination, intolerance and division in the society. Above all, the broadcaster's lifestyle, personality, and social standing should be without blemish if his enviable ranking as a celebrity and role model in society is to be sustained. This is because what we preach on radio and television; our voices on radio; our faces on television, go farther and wider than we can never imagine. These voices, names and images in the minds of the listeners or viewers present larger than life pictures that result in the interpretation of the roles of the broadcaster in various forms and dimensions. The broadcaster is seen as one who mingles, wines and dines with the high and mighty in society and, therefore, in a position to move mountains. This is one public perception that puts the broadcaster on the edge in the discharge of his functions to the society. The societal pressure is more with friends and family members whose demands have no limits. The broadcaster is expected to live in expensive homes, drive big cars, and wear expensive clothing. They feel that the broadcaster should demonstrate affluence befitting of the status of his profession.

Eminent people like presidents, governors, legislators and captains of commerce and industry who interact freely with the broadcaster on public issues on radio and television also share this false perception arising from this societal pressure.

However, many broadcasters that I know and worked with in my years in the industry were neither equipped nor prepared to play these and other roles which the profession has clearly bestowed on them. The first challenge in this regard is the condition of service. In the broadcasting industry, the take-home pay cannot take the broadcaster home, no matter how prudent he/she may be. While poor salaries and remunerations for the broadcasters in the public-owned broadcast media organizations may not generate grumblings and complaints, those in the private media are not even sure to get the stipends at the end of the month.

When I joined the profession as a young recruit in Enugu in the early 1980s, three of us in that generation and about the same age; Vinmartin Obiora Ilo, Barikumo Adou and I, decided to pull our meagre resources together to rent a 3-bedroom flat at Achara Layout, a medium density part of the Enugu metropolis.

The decision came about because none of us could afford to rent a flat which then cost One hundred and twenty naira per month (less than $100 per month). By our arrangements, each of us had a room while we shared the living room and other facilities. We also shared the rent equally. But as days and months went by, it became clear that we could not pay as and when due. One of us must default each month, most times on clear genuine reasons known to all the parties.

Unfortunately, we had a caretaker who was very unfriendly and had zero interest in any story but the rent. To make matters worse, our caretaker's wife had a shop at the gate from where she used to monitor our movement and passed the information to the husband, the caretaker. In front of the shop, on a piece of paper, was a display of all occupants of the building and their financial status on rents, electricity and water bills. In our case, the caretaker displayed our names in such a way that passers-by, as well as anyone who came to buy anything in the shop, must see the undignifyng information. At that time, the three of us were very popular household names in Enugu in particular and most Eastern states in general, because of our regular voices on news and programmes on Radio Nigeria.

When all efforts to persuade the caretaker to remove the list from the shop and give us time to pay failed, Vinmartin suggested we make every effort to locate the landlord, the actual owner of the property, wherever he might be. In Vinmartin's argument, the landlord may be a more compassionate person to deal with. When we eventually met the landlord in his home in another part of Enugu, he granted us audience and demanded to know what we did for a living. "I am Vinmartin Ilo of Radio

Nigeria." The landlord screamed and stood up to embrace Vin! The landlord, a man in his late 60s, was an ardent listener of radio. As he hosted us, his radio was by his side with one of our recorded programmes running. Before the dust settled, Vin introduced me, then introduced Barikumo. At that point, the landlord, unaware of our mission, decided to invite his wife and the household to come and meet the personalities behind the voices they hear on radio. The reception we received was so impressive that we didn't know how to begin the story of our mission. We were ashamed to say that we, these top radio personalities, were owing rent in his house, and needed a waiver! It was a moment when we realized why a profession like broadcasting needs to be well-renumerated as found in developed countries. The detail of what later transpired during our encounter with the landlord is a story for another day.

But suffice is to say that in the course of time, all the three of us later rose to high ranking positions in broadcasting by a combination of these factors – discipline, dedication, patience, hardwork and regular self-development. Many years later, Vinmartin Obiora Ilo was to later become Special Adviser to the Governor of Enugu State on Media Relations. Before that appointment, he was Executive Director at Daar Communications and responsible for African Independent Television's South Eastern operations. As I write, Barikumo Adou is currently General Manager, Radio Nigeria Uyo, Akwa Ibom State. Until this development,

Bari had also served as General Manager, Salt FM, Abakaliki, Ebonyi State. These early life experiences influenced the hard choices we made in order to be successful in the profession.

To avoid the kind of encounter with the landlord that I just narrated, a broadcaster needs to work harder to established some form of basic financial freedom and stability. When a broadcaster is involved in petty and sundary debts all over the place, within and outside the broadcasting house, it affects the reputation of the organization, undermines the credibility of its message to the society. And this culture is common in the broadcasting industry.

However, I am delighted that many broadcasters in Nigeria today have broken the chains of poverty through self-development and the exploration of the privileges of industry. The list of broadcasters in this special category is long. And it has continued to grow.

A broadcaster must also be neat and smartly dressed all the time, be well comported, show discipline and be compliant to public order. As a broadcaster, it is difficult to know who knows you. There is no hiding place. Therefore, common shameful habits that we think do not matter should be avoided because our job keeps us under watch by the society.

We should be interested in humanitarian work, social development issues and community development initiatives in our environments. Besides, a broadcaster should be a model in maintaining good family life.

Chapter 4

Reporting for the Broadcast Media

Reporting for radio can be quite challenging, but more often than not, interesting. This is because, radio reporting requires exceptional creativity, dynamism, imagination, command of language, voice talent, fluency, eloquence, in-depth knowledge of the issues, firm understanding of the target audience, and presentation skills. A radio (or television) reporter must be quick to react to unexpected events, and even quicker to think on his or her feet. These attributes are essentially driven by basic studio infrastructure built on solid engineering transmission facilities that guarantee clear sound signals required in the broadcasting value chain to get the message across.

Absence of these qualities and conditions can create a a huge challenge. Aside from possessing the above-mentioned qualities, which could be acquired through learning, training, exposure or self-development, the radio reporter has to master brevity, conciseness and correctness in the message and delivery. A reporter must learn that the message from radio ought to be simple, short, clear and straight to the point.

All activities, both for news and programmes operations in broadcasting are time-specific in take-off, duration and landing, hence the need for them to be comprehensive, direct, short and simple; rendered with the fluent language, friendly voice, capable of catching the attention and interest of the listener who indeed depends on the voice, content and presentation style to make any meaning out of what the reporter is saying. In radio broadcast, time is not only important, it is everything.

Against this background, from my field experiences, reporting for radio is therefore like describing a situation to the blind that cannot see but has a right to know, feel, experience and possibly participate in the event, system or process. As a blind medium, radio programmes and information have to be interesting, inviting, and catchy with dependable information presented with every clarity and simplicity in a manner that brings the listener fully into comprehensive understanding and appreciation of the issues and conversation. The reporter therefore must be well informed about the issues, the activity and the content of the programme, objectives, desired benefits and impacts to society in order to be in a position to inform others.

Above all, who are your audience, what are their interests and does your report contain vital information and data that satisfies these interests and expectations of the listener? The information disseminated through the radio must be true, dependable and verifiable. The listener has every faith, trust and confidence that information from the radio is the truth and nothing but the truth. This is a public trust vested in the broadcast media that every radio or television station strives to do nothing to breach. Over the years, I was involved in striving to uphold this burden of trust and basic ethics while serving the Federal Radio Corporation of Nigeria as a broadcaster and journalist.

While school provided the education and knowledge, much of the experiences were gained sometimes by jumping straight into an ocean with little or no swimming skills. As a firm believer in the popular saying that the taste of the pudding is in the eating, I found it more rewarding putting theory into practice at any slightest opportunity.

For instance, on 23rd March, 1994, I reported for duty like every other day and was informed that the Director, News Division, Patrick Obazele, was looking for me and had left an instruction that I see him urgently. I tried to think of what offence I might have committed. Invitation by any Director of News to a common Reporter can be a double-edged sword during my days as a reporter in the Radio Nigeria Network News Team. The outcomes were usually unpredictable. I summoned up courage and raced to Chief Obazele's office."good afternoon sir," I greeted as I stood before him. He ignored my greetings, lifted up his

47

face from a document he was vetting, stared at me with a very stern face, paused for a while and then roared, "My friend, do you have an international passport?" he queried. "Yes sir," I answered in subdued and trembling voice. The demand by Chief Obazele was most timely and surprising.

A few weeks ago, Sunny Odunwo, the then Chief Press Secretary to Colonel Raji Rasaki, the Governor of Lagos State at the time, "granted general amnesty" to all members of the Lagos State Government House Press Corps by securing international passport for all. The gesture was his own approach to media relations, "his own strategy to sustain the reporters' goodwill." Chief Obazele continued, "... get me the passport immediately and prepare to go to India to cover an assignment." "Thank you sir," I responded and bowed out of his office. I left his office pondering on what the trip was all about. What assignment? I queried in my mind.

I arrived in New Delhi, India on 30th March, 1994 for the assignment with little or no information on the objective of the summit, the goal of the G.15 as a world body, Nigeria's interest in the organization and the links with Nigeria's foreign policy. I had also no information on the structure of the conference, the likely participants and other details that a reporter needs to know in advance before proceeding to an important assignment of that global importance.

At that time, the internet culture in developing countries was virtually non-existent especially in Nigeria. Since it was my first international assignment, I also lacked the experience which a reporter requires under such a circumstance to 'squeeze water out of stone'. I therefore went to India without adequate information and knowledge of the assignment for which I was expected to report, inform and educate the public on its proceedings and outcome. Sending out an inexperienced reporter with little or no information to important assignments is one common mistake media organizations make with far reaching negative consequences on the quality of reports, the content and delivery, resulting in the audience not getting the message.

On arrival at the Taj Mahal Hotel India, I was exposed to the accreditation procedure which essentially is the first step for a reporter sent to cover an assignment, especially outside the country. The accreditation is required to put the reporter's name on the participant's register and obtain a conference identity card for easy access to the conference venue and facilities.

At the accreditation point, delegates were issued with conference material. The material therefore became the initial access to detailed information on the summit. From the material, I came to learn that members of G.15 include Algeria, Argentina, Brazil, Chile, Egypt, India, and Indonesia. Others are Islamic Republic of Iran, Jamaica, Kenya, Malaysia, Mexico, Senegal, Sri Lanka, Bolivia, Venezuela Zimbabwe and Nigeria.

The Group of Fifteen (G-15) was established by fifteen developing countries during the 9th Summit of the Non-Aligned Movement held in Belgrade in September 1989. The group was conceived as a small cohesive body of

49

developing countries with sufficient economic and political weight to make authoritative pronouncements reflecting their common standpoint on the major developments in the world economy and international economic relations. The goal of the G-15 was to be recognized as a logical dialogue partner of the Group of 7 (G-7, now G-8) highly industrialized countries.

The G-15 members therefore share common positions on world economic policy issues. But the Heads of State and Government of the group decided that, in addition to this broader purpose, the G-15 would also take up projects which could bring direct benefits to the peoples of the member States, which could help in enhancing the credibility of the group, inspire confidence among its member States, thereby strengthening its unity and cohesion. This, it was expected, could enhance the bargaining power of the group in dealing with developed countries.

The G-15 was established on the firm belief of the considerable potential for greater and mutually beneficial cooperation among developing countries, especially in the areas of investment, trade and technology. It was also expected to become a catalyst for greater South-South cooperation, to pursue a more positive and productive North-South dialogue. As such, it was envisaged that the G-15 will serve as a forum for regular consultations among developing countries with a view to coordinating policies and actions of South-South countries at the global level, and assist in the formulation and implementation of programmes of cooperation.

As at 1994, the contribution of G-15 countries to global crude oil output stood at 25% with Iran, Mexico, Venezuela, Nigeria, Brazil and Algeria being among the world's leading producers of oil and natural gas. Other member countries were abundantly endowed with extractive resources such as copper (Chile): nickel and tin (Indonesia); sugar (Brazil, India); tea (India, Kenya, Sri Lanka); coffee (Brazil); cocoa (Indonesia, Nigeria, Brazil); rubber (Indonesia, Malaysia); cassava (Nigeria, Brazil, Indonesia) and oil-seeds (Brazil, Argentina).

Some have relatively developed economies with large diversified industrial bases (Brazil, India, Mexico), developed infrastructure (Chile, Malaysia) and advanced technological capabilities in critical areas like pharmaceuticals (Argentina, Brazil, India) and information technology (Malaysia, India, Argentina). Since 1994, the G-15 countries accounted for one-third of the world's population, 27% of total exports and 30% of total imports of goods and services by developing countries. In terms of GDP size, 12 member countries counted among the world's 50 biggest economies, with three (India, Brazil, Mexico) ranking among the biggest 15. Six G-15 countries (Brazil, Mexico, Chile, India, Malaysia, Argentina) ranked among the top 30 destinations for foreign direct investment, and three (Malaysia, Chile, India) figured among the first 30 countries on the global competitiveness index. It was in anticipation of these progressive contributions to the World economy that the 1994 India Summit was taken very seriously.

At the Conference Centre, I ran into the officials of Nigerian High Commission in New Delhi who were coordinating the event with officials of the Nigerian Foreign Ministry who I could not track down in Nigeria as a result of the lateness of my nomination to cover the event. The meeting offered me the opportunity to pour out some of my frustrations and challenges.

Both the officials of the High Commission and the Foreign Ministry were quite helpful in resolving my immediate concerns – where to send my stories from, structure and information on the conference, history and composition of Nigeria delegation as well as Nigeria's interest in the summit. I clutched closely to some of the friendly officials, made friends with them as they bought into my problems and proffered solutions as best as they could. The intervention was just timely and largely divine.

By 12 noon in New Delhi, the opening ceremony of the summit was all over. I joined the Embassy officials in their vehicle to the Nigerian High Commission where I was given free telephone lines and fax machines to file my story. As at 1994, internet and information communication technology was unknown to any average reporter in Nigeria, most developing countries and the sub-Saharan Africa. Reporting and broadcasting were more traditional and analogue-based.

By 12 noon in India, it was just 7.30am in Nigeria. So I had sufficient time at the High Commission to develop my story and a correspondent's report. It was a tradition for most reporters on radio, especially Radio Nigeria, to do at least two reports when they are sent out on very important assignments. The first and major report is a voice report which we referred to as Correspondent's Report. The correspondent's report, among other benefits, establishes beyond doubt the credibility of the broadcast media, that its reporter is or was physically on ground at the event.

The correspondent's report therefore takes the listener directly to the scene of the event through actualities, sights and sounds, voices of participants and behind the scene events which the listeners cannot appreciate in the main story referred to in broadcasting as "hard news". The correspondent's report allows the reporter to describe the environment, the preparations, the arrivals and reception of delegates, the quality of attendance, the sequence of events, agreements and disagreements at the meetings, the opportunities and lessons, among others.

On the other hand, the main story or Hard News is developed from mainly key speeches, pronouncements and decisions from the conference. In developing the story, the reporter has the responsibility to ensure that the Hard News are in line with the editorial policy, expectation and interest of the organization, citizens and country the reporter represents before any other consideration. Since it was my first international outing, I did not know if my first story (Hard News) from the summit reproduced below met this expectation.

53

"The Federal Government says its interest in joining the G.15 is to expand its trade and investment opportunities in member countries.

The Head of State, General Sani Abacha, gave the clarification today in New Delhi India while addressing the Opening Session of the G.15 Summit.

General Abacha explained that at a time when the global economy was under the rigid control of rich and powerful nations under the G.7, the poor and developing nations have no option than to come together and explore opportunities within their countries.

He added that Nigeria's commitment to G.15 will continue to depend on the ability of the group to address the increasing gap between the rich and poor nations in world trade and investments.

Earlier, the Prime Minister of India, Narasima Rao, had called for closer cooperation between member countries of G.15 to address the common problems of poverty, ignorance, illiteracy and conflicts common in member countries.

The India Prime Minister attributed the worsening economic conditions of developing countries to the dominance of rich and powerful nations in the global economy."

Correspondent Report (Intro)

"The G.15 Summit has opened in New Delhi India.

The Head of State, General Sani Abacha is leading Nigeria delegation to the Summit.

Radio Nigeria Correspondent Orji Ogbonnaya Orji who is covering the summit is on the line from New Delhi.

The group G.15 is a group of 15 countries drawn mainly from poor and developing nations with similar economic problems and challenges of development. They include Nigeria, India, Egypt, Jamaica, Malaysia, Singapore, Algeria, Argentina, Brazil, Chile, and Indonesia. Others are Islamic Republic of Iran, Jamaica, Kenya, Mexico, Senegal, Sri Lanka, Bolivia, Venezuela and Zimbabwe.

The objective of the group is to find ways and means of advancing the economic interests of the member countries and citizens through trade and investments in the world economy dominated by rich and powerful nations under the G.7.

The Summit in India is focusing on trade and investment opportunities in power, energy, oil and gas, agriculture, telecommunications, construction industry, banking and finance and how investors from member countries could be encouraged to fully explore these opportunities to boost their economic fortunes. This probably explained why investors, captains of commerce and industry drawn from these major sectors dominated the list of delegates from most member countries including Nigeria.

Presenting Nigeria's core interest as a member of the global organization, the Head of State, General Sani Abacha urged investors from Nigeria and member countries to seize what he called a golden opportunity...

Cue in: (the voice insert comes in...) "Nigeria is here in India."

Cue out: (voice inserts ends)... "For the benefit of our governments and citizens."

Earlier, the Prime Minister of the host nation, Narasima Rao, used the forum to launch a comprehensive economic plan for India and invited all member countries to use the plan to invest in what he described as India's walk to economic prosperity.

Cue in: (the Indian Prime Minister's voice starts-"Our plan is targeted at...

Cue out: (the voice ends) – "leading to economic recovery."

The Indian Prime Minister added that the economic plan will lead his country to prosperity and trade advantage in the health sector, information and communication technology.

Over 150 delegates drawn from 15 member countries of the organization are attending the summit expected to end in two days' time.

This is Orji Ogonnaya Orji reporting from New Delhi, India.

With the Hard News and the Correspondent's Report with the voice inserts programmed (cued)ready, I picked the telephone line at the Nigeria High Commission and was through to the news room in Ikoyi, Lagos.

"Hello! This is Orji from New Delhi," and everyone in the news room began to run from pillar to post to ensure I received immediate attention by taking the Hard News by Fax and the correspondent's report through recording. It was a very important but unwritten law in the Network News Room to give reporters and correspondents very high priority once they come on line so as to save telephone bills. Any Staff in the news room, who ignored an incoming report from the field, or delays the report unnecessarily on the line, faces severe sanctions if the reporter or correspondent makes a formal report on return from the trip.

But at that time, the news room was indeed a family, full of humour, where everyone felt happy and ready to get the job done. The reporter on tour also has a responsibility of embracing the culture that we called "address the press" on return from a trip. The culture involved sharing gifts and souvenirs brought from the country of visit; no stories or excuses. It was no bribery but a culture that reduced acrimony between reporters on the field and editorial staff on the desk.

On that first assignment, I was equally exposed to the importance of a reporter being very aware and conscious of the news deadline of the organization he represents, either on national or international assignment. A news deadline is the time in which a reporter's story must reach the newsroom if such a story will form part of the major news and programmes of the organization. Another important lesson from that assignment was the need for the reporter to find out, identify and obtain valid information and data about the delegation representing his country, the leader of that delegation, the country's national interest in the event and the specific news angles that satisfies the interest of the reporter's organization. In the same direction, who are the other big players in the event whose interests and positions matter? This information at the disposal of the reporter will help shape the story.

As at the time of writing this book and this particular chapter (January 21st, 2014), the 2014 World Economic Forum in Davos, Switzerland was just beginning. Channels Television, one of Nigeria's broadcast media that I find quite interesting, had dispatched a reporter, one Harriet Agbeyi, to Davos to cover the event. I watched this reporter filing a pre-event report on Channels. She gave a good profile of activities expected at the event and the expectations from the conference. Her report largely addressed the issues of proximity, national and citizens' interest in the global forum, President Jonathan's participation at the event and the implications for Nigeria's overall economic interest. Although the report was not quite audible, it was good in terms of content.

As the only radio reporter in the Nigerian delegation to the summit of the G.15 held in India in March 1994, I left Nigeria for the assignment with everything but information and data. This is a common mistake among reporters from developing countries. The India trip was a great exposure to the consequences of such mistakes. But the challenges and lessons became handy in contending with the real issues in reporting, especially for the broadcast media.

News and Programmes Beats in Broadcasting

News and programme operations in broadcasting, like any other media activities, are broken down into Beats for effective coverage of the areas of operation of the broadcasting organisation. The beats are also essential in exposing reporters, especially new entrants, to the various and often critical areas of the station's news and programmes divisions. Secondly, this enables the station to build professionalism among the corps of the news and programmes staff in specific areas of operations to the extent that over time such reporters or producers become reliable resource persons and authority in their respective assigned beats.

In this context therefore, news and programmes beats are specific areas of interest and operation assigned to a reporter or producer for purposes of daily news and information sources, coverage and reporting for sustained benefit of the broadcast organization. The reporters specifically assigned to manage the beats are themselves known as correspondents.

The FRCN news and programmes operations over the years embraced this module as a culture in news management and programmes operations. I also know that the BBC, VOA and other international and local media have built this culture as an important part of their operations. In the process, some beats have become well known and common in most broadcasting media organizations. The beats are as many as the organization may decide from time to time. Below are some of them:

- State House/Government House – covers the activities of the President of the Country, Heads of Government and State Governors in the States.

- Politics – concerned with coverage of activities of political parties, political activities, electoral commissions and allied events.

- Defense & Security – reports all Defense and Security issues, the armed forces, paramilitary agencies and crime related issues.

- Legislature – covers the activities of National and State Assemblies, legislative matters and similar issues related with legislations.

- Judiciary – covers the judiciary, court proceedings, the Bar, the Bench and associated legal matters of public interest.

- Aviation– Covers aviation industry developments, airports administration, air transportation and allied matters.

- Sports – covers sports, athletics, industry organizations and other related issues.

- Economy – largely interested in all economic matters such as banking and finance policies, tax, revenue administration, stock and securities, debt management, etc.

- Health – reports health related issues, medicine, hospital activities, and pharmaceutical research.

- General – Reporters on general beat operate in a pool and can be assigned to any event that is available and not covered by a correspondent.

During my career, I covered many beats as a correspondent, they include Government House Lagos State, Aviation, politics, National Assembly and the Presidency. Each beat has its politics which is similar and sometimes comparable to the rivalry between the People's Democratic Party (PDP) and All Peoples Congress (APC).

In all the beats, each correspondent struggles to assert the influence and relevance of the media organization the correspondent represents. There is also the politics of recognition and acceptance by other stakeholders in the beat, and the strive for recognition by the Media Relations Officers of the institutions that make up the beat.

The most common is the rivalry among the reporters, the conspiracy against each other, and the struggles for virtually every opportunity as well as the "fight" over who gets what and how. A reporter must be prepared for beat politics and struggles. It is a factor a reporter cannot ignore. The experience of a reporter in each beat is sometimes similar but in most cases, unique and diverse.

Chapter 5

Reporting Politics, Political Parties, Campaigns and Elections

The political beat is perhaps one of the most interesting and dynamic beats any reporter would want to be assigned to as a journalist. I moved from aviation to political beat at a time when the Babangida Administration had decreed only two political parties for Nigeria. These were the Social Democratic Party (SDP) and the National Republican Convention (NRC). While Alhaji Babagana Kingibe was the national chairman of the Social Democratic Party, Chief Tom Ikimi led the National Republican Convention as its national chairman. The headquarters of the SDP was at 9, Ademola Street, SW Ikoyi. It was later moved to the complex currently being occupied by the National Defense College in Abuja.

I was assigned to cover the SDP as Radio Nigeria political correspondent while my friend and colleague, Gbenga Onayiga was assigned to report the NRC. Both Gbenga and I were required to jointly cover the National Electoral Commission(NEC), the electoral umpire at the time. NEC, as it was called then, was under the chairmanship of Prof. Humphrey Nwosu, a political science professor from the University of Nigeria, Nsukka.

The generations of reporters I met on the political beat and worked very closely with at that time currently occupy the very top echelon of Nigerian media today. They include, but are not limited to, former presidential spokesman and current chairman of Thisday editorial board, Segun Adeniyi, who, at that time, reports for the Concord Newspapers group; the former Managing Director of Thisday Newspapers who currently is Chief Executive of The Nation Newspapers, Victor Ifijeh. At that time, Victor too was in the Concord group.

Others were Tunde Rahman, now editor, ThisDay on Sunday; Ralph Egbu, who served Abia State Government several times as Press Secretary, as Commissioner for Information and then rose to become Secretary to the Abia State Government, and the former Special Assistant to the President of the Senate; Emeka Nwosu, who at that time was political editor of the Daily Times; Akin Onipede of The Tribune, who is currently a Deputy Director, Public Affairs, at the Nigerian Tourism Development Corporation; Dapo Ogunwusi who rose to become the Editor in Chief of The Tribune; Martins Oloja, who is currently Editor of The Guardian.

We were a very solid group of disciplined, professional and progressive corps of journalists who used the platform to define our respective future in the profession. I can proudly say that I cannot remember any in that generation who has not made a positive mark today in the industry.

In reporting political parties, a reporter has the important job of carefully studying the philosophy of the party, if one exists, the party constitution, the party manifesto; and most importantly, the party organs and structure at all levels - federal, state, local government, down to the ward levels. A political correspondent, especially one who reports for the broadcast media also has to study the meaning and importance of the party slogans, symbols, mission and vision. There is also need for him to know the various electoral laws, rules and regulations that guide political activities and activism.

Beyond this, the political correspondent needs to be fully educated and informed about the leadership structure and organs of administration of the national and state electoral institutions and the limit of their functions and powers. Far more important is the need to know the major politicians on first name basis, their phone numbers and important details about them. From my experience as a political correspondent, I do not know how any reporter can cope and report politics effectively without these vital information, knowledge and cobweb of contacts.

This is because political activities are quite difficult to regulate, streamline, and coordinate in a manner that gives the reporter an idea of where important stories would come from. In most situations, political activities are all over the place, in the open and in secret. The secret and very late meetings and consultations are where important decisions are reached. And if the reporter has close relations with key and influential members of the party, he may get informaion on the decisions made even before the meeting is over!

One secret of gaining the confidence, attention and respect of politicians is to ensure visibility and prompt attendance at all meetings and events, irrespective of timing and proximity. I made this a personal project while reporting the Social Democratic Party, SDP.

I recall that several months after I joined the beat, the National Chairman of the Party, Babagana Kingibe, neither knew me in person nor did I have access to him or his contacts until he saw me at an emergency National Consultative Forum held in Kano in 1992. At that time, the party was facing serious crises over heavy dusts generated by its party primaries. The controversies held the party leadership at the throat. Thus, series of Consultative Fora were convened to resolve the disputes. The one held in Kano was so sudden that most prominent members of the party missed the meeting but I was among the very few correspondents that attended. The Press Secretary to the National Chairman, Simon Ebulu, who indeed was my reliable contact and confidant and who also normally coordinated such meetings was surprisingly absent. This was quite strange to me.

During the press conference that followed, when the National Chairman saw me placing my microphone before him, struggling and pushing in the midst of Kano-based journalists, he recognised me as the reporter he sees at every party event in any part of the country and regularly at the party headquarters, then in Ademola Street, Ikoyi, Lagos. He immediately beckoned to me. "You came all the way from Lagos?" he asked, "Yes sir!" I replied. "Good, please coordinate the Press Conference," the chairman directed. "Yes sir," I bowed with excitement, following a sudden elevation from a common reporter to a 'proxy media assistant to the national chairman'.

Even though my elevation was temporary, I immediately considered it a prime opportunity that must be fully explored in order to get closer to the Chairman in view of future benefits. Thus, I did as requested, gently collecting the microphone and greeting the party leadership, gentlemen of the Press, and generally making everyone in the hall aware of my new assignment and the guidelines for the Press conference. I thereafter requested the National Chairman to make his introductory remarks after which I called for questions from the media.

There was no doubt that I did well as the Chairman and the party leadership commended my work. After that assignment, I became well-known and somehow close to the SDP Chairman, Alhaji Babagana Kingibe, during his tenure and later as one of the Presidential Aspirants on the platform of the Party. The relationship enhanced my authority, influence, visibility and competence.

Another secret of being an outstanding reporter for the political beat is to ensure excellent quality of reports. The politicians and their supporters pay close attention to the broadcast media and for the print media, they read and even document them. I realized this when I wrote a News Analysis on the SDP Governorship Primaries and the chances of the party in the elections. The news analysis was broadcast on the Network News of Radio Nigeria at the peak of the SDP internal crisis in 1992. In my view, I thought I was fair and balanced. But I didn't know that I touched the tiger's tail. The high and mighty within the leadership of the party were uncomfortable with my conclusions and called for my head. Some even made their way to my office to ask for my immediate redeployment. The controversy kept me off the Party Secretariat for two weeks to allow the dust settle. It was the intervention of the Party National Publicity Secretary, David Iornem, and the then National Secretary of the party, Alexis Anielo, that helped to calm frayed nerves, after which I sneaked back into the beat.

However, the incident made me even more popular and visible on the beat. However, I found politicians the most willing, dependable and friendly sources of information largely because of interests for or against their political aspirations. Every politician finds the media quite an important tool available for use to either frustrate or further personal or group interests as events unfold in the political space. As a political correspondent, the task is to find out what the key issues are and for whose interest, and then situate the issues appropriately. It is also the responsibility of the reporter to weigh these issues on the scale of public interest, balance and fairness within the framework of the prevailing regulations, guidelines and the law. This will help the listeners make responsible political decisions.

From their varied experiences on the beat, political reporters in the print media are more adventurous in this direction. They enjoy appreciably relative freedom, less editorial control, more space and editorial freedom to operate and of course, they compete for better attention in the market. The electronic media do not compete at that time as ownership was still rigidly held by only government. The deregulation of the industry has opened doors for competition between the private and public owned media organisations. But are the public funded media organisations in a position to compete without reforms?

As earlier highlighted, understanding the key issues, the key players, the leadership structure and organs of administration in the political arena and sending proper feedback to the media organization that the reporter represents, in a timely and professional manner, are critical success factors in the work of the political correspondent. One of the key players that a political correspondent must contend with is the fellow reporter and correspondent on the same beat. Political reporters and correspondents are as slippery, unreliable and flexible as politicians. You can hardly depend on one another where the issue of date and venue of important assignments, exclusive stories, professional interests and relationship with key players are concerned. Even your closest colleague on the beat will abandon you. The culture in political reporting at the time therefore was more of, everyone to himself and God for us all, reporters on the beat operate in secret and have very powerful caucuses just like the politicians. They hardly trust one another.

As part of efforts to promote discipline, cooperation, self-development, professional regulation, learning, knowledge sharing and capacity development within and among journalists deployed to report politics, the correspondents at that time came together and formed what we called the National Association of Political Correspondents (NAPOC). It was largely Lagos-based. I was among the founding members. Emeka Nwosu of the Daily Times was the Chairman.

The Association(NAPOC) became a platform to seek support and partnership with institutions and organizations in areas of professional exposure, training and manpower development. Such important organizations like the National Orientation Agency, political parties, the Federal Ministry of Information, Embassies and High Commissions helped at that initial stage to build the capacity of reporters on the beat so as to deepen democratic culture and political education in a nation just emerging from 29 years of military rule.

Again, an uninformed political correspondent will not be able to effectively source and develop stories whose content makes meaning to an audience who desperately need the information to make the right choices.

Coverage of Party Primaries and Political Campaigns

Party Primaries are internal elections or selection process within a political party to choose the most suitable candidate that would carry the party's flag in a scheduled general election. Unlike the general election where all registered voters are eligible to vote, only delegates carefully elected at the congresses of the party are eligible to vote at the primaries.

Party primaries are important for the political reporter. The public interest each aspirant would have generated either negatively or positively, as well as the consequences on governance, usually attracts deserved media attention as part of the build-up to the party primaries. The more influential, and controversial the aspirants are, the more the media attention and commentary they attract. This is in addition to social commentaries, debates, public discussions, analyses and political calculations by both the electorate and the competing parties in the election.

It is the aspirant elected or selected in the party primaries that becomes the candidate for the party. While aspirants are elected or selected in the primaries, it is candidates that represent the party in the general elections. I find it quite disturbing to read political stories and see reporters not being able to differentiate between an aspirant to a political position and a candidate of the party. It is important that the report follows the trail of issues and keep same constantly in the front burner in the public domain and in people's consciousness as the countdown to the party primaries begins.

Therefore, coverage of the primaries is essential to providing the electorate with timely, comprehensive and correct information on the plurality of choices available to the electorate as chosen by the parties from the primaries. The reports from the primaries on the process of selection or election, the background, personality, track record, vision and philosophy of each candidate and how each of them intends to execute the party's manifesto for the benefit of the citizens, are issues that engage the political reporter's interest.

The conduct of party primaries is usually done by the respective parties, using their own generated guidelines. The reporter is expected to present the issues in a fair, objective, balanced, analytical and constructive approach. Looking back, I recall the coverage of the SDP Presidential Primaries held at Jos Township Stadium.

The Presidential Primaries was the climax of series of political meetings, hues and cries, complaints and explanations, petitions and recourse mechanisms, consultations, calculations, agreements and disagreements that trailed the decision of the National Chairman of the Party, Alhaji Babagana Kingibe and an international businessman and well-known philanthropist, Chief M.K.O Abiola, to run for the Presidential post under the platform of the Social Democratic Party. Although there were many other aspirants such as Alhaji Atiku Abubakar, but Kingibe and Abiola generated most interest in the national and international media.

The presidential aspirations of these two powerful figures made the SDP presidential primaries in Jos very tense and contentious. This was because it was one of the most outstanding political party events of the transition to civil rule ochestrated by the military regime of General Ibrahim Babangida. Little public attention was focused in the direction of the other political party, National Republican Convention presidential primaries between Alhaji Bashir Tofa and others which held simultaneously in Port Harcourt. The Kingibe, Abiola, Atiku contest was more interesting and action-packed.

I arrived in Jos to cover the event two days ahead of the primaries. It was one assignment that I always love to remember. From Hill Station Hotel in Jos, the venue of the accreditation, I had a first-hand view and observed that the world media were ready for the event. The arguments were for Abiola or Kingibe. While Abiola's problem was not money but how to spend it, Kingibe was reputed to have the party structure and machinery firmly in his grip. Besides, 12 out of 18 SDP governors and their delegates were said to have endorsed Kingibe's bid.

On the other hand, Atiku Abubakar was said to be on standby to pull the rug from under the feet of either the candidates if the situation threw him up as what politicians in the context refer to as "beautiful bride". For the correspondents, stories were everywhere and from every angle. It required a wide network of contacts, penetration, knowledge of the beat, dynamism and resilience to source fresh angles to any story as events unfolded every minute, every second and from every angle in Jos.

With over 10,000 accredited delegates, millions of supporters, and hangers-on, all hotels in Jos and neighboring hotels in Bauchi were fully booked. We reporters moved from one hotel to another to remain on top of latest developments. The first and second nights before the primaries witnessed door to door campaigns to persuade delegates to various camps with, sometimes, irresistible offers.

Political jobbers, touts and hangers-on were also all over the hotel lobbies in Jos, trading freely on rumour, cheap blackmail, propaganda and humour. These and other distractions constituted nuisance during the convention. However, these are part of the side effects to political reporting. In spite of the huge gathering of political heavy-weights in Jos, there were no killing, kidnappings, assassination, acid attacks, or any of the mayhem that often attended Nigerian political events. Everyone tried to win attention and vote through argument, persuasion, lobbying, propaganda and other legitimate forms of engagement.

Back to my story, the Radio Nigeria Network News Room ran a 24 hours service as developments unfolded. Gbenga and I kept the nation updated of unfolding events from Jos and Port Harcourt, venues of the presidential primaries of both parties. I worked with a team of Radio Nigeria Correspondents from Kaduna and Enugu - John Aduku and Okechukwu Anakudo respectively.

As a political reporter on such a complex assignment, my duties on arrival were to:

74

- Identify the main venue of accreditation.
- Identify the major centers of action, where all the key players were staying.
- Find out how I could have access to information on the outcome of meetings before the convention.
- Identify my competitors.
- Ask myself– which of the media houses covering this assignment was likely to beat me to breaking a story by simple reason of deadline?
- Ask myself what the coverage of such media are? How can I mitigate the risk of my organization getting the real story from an alternative source? A reporter who is not conscious of getting the story across to the editor as fast as possible is not good enough. For the radio reporter, time is of the essence. For this important assignment under discussion, I quickly identified the BBC and VOA as my closest competitors.

At that time, Radio Nigeria Network News enjoyed monopoly in national coverage. All State-owned radio stations depended on the Radio Nigeria Network News and the BBC for stories. I then made friends with Shola Odunfa, the BBC correspondent who was leading the team of BBC and other foreign correspondent who were in Jos for the event. I monitored their movements and asked some crafty questions to ascertain their deadlines and plans to file stories. But while Shola and the BBC team were equipped with modern gadgets to file their stories from any point at any time, I was equipped with none and had to depend on taxi to Nigeria Telecommunications Office in Jos for access to telephone lines. I could not afford the cost of telephone bills in the hotel.

On the day of the convention, there were different stories based on several speeches. But all attention was on who will win the primaries and become the SDP presidential candidate. The outcome of the primaries between Abiola, Kingibe and Atiku was all that mattered.

After the first round of voting, the men had been separated from the boys. It was a clear direct contest between Abiola and Kingibe. In the spirit of fair contest, Atiku withdrew from the race and directed his supporters and loyal delegates to back Abiola against Kingibe as the last two got set for the second and final round of voting. This decision was not in public but I got the information as Atiku made the decision.

At that time, Atiku Abubakar was a younger, emerging, but very articulate promising politician. In 1993, he was certainly a lightweight compared to Abiola and Kingibe. As counting progressed, and as a reporter curious and anxious to break the story that the whole nation was waiting for, I used the privilege of that scoop and reasoned that Abiola had won even before anyone cast a ballot. But the question was with what margin? I immediately put a taxi on standby as I began to draft my story in readiness for 4 p.m news which was about an hour ahead. When I observed that Abiola's votes had surpassed that of Kingibe by a big margin, I sneaked out of the stadium, boarded the taxi and headed straight to NITEL. At NITEL, I dialed the news room where the entire staff on duty were anxiously waiting for the story for the 4 p.m news which was just 17 minutes away and I faxed my story, reproduced below:

> *Chief MKO Abiola has been elected the Presidential Candidate of the Social Democratic Party SDP.*
>
> *Chief Abiola defeated the former National Chairman of the Party Alhaji Babagana Kingibe in a keenly contested election decided by over 10,000 party delegates.*
>
> *Radio Nigeria political correspondent, Orji Ogbonnaya Orji, in Jos reports that Alhaji Atiku Abubakar who withdrew from the race after the first round of voting enhanced Abiola's victory with his supporters at the second and final round of voting.*
>
> *Other details of the SDP presidential party primaries will come to you in our subsequent bulletin.*

As soon as the story broke out through the powerful inviting velvet voice of the late Zakari Mohammed, the nation went into jubilation. I learnt that MKO Abiola supporters took to the streets in open celebration.

I never cared about the margin with which Abiola won because time to me was more important. Above all, what mattered most to listeners at that time was who won? While the counting was on, my story was already on the 4 p.m bulletin. Professionally, I took a risk but it was a reasonable and comfortable one which any resilient reporter must be ready to take under certain circumstances. I felt fulfilled that I broke the story.

Effective coverage of party primaries is important because it sets the stage and the right tone for the listeners to be able to depend on and trust the broadcast medium, knowing that it has an effective reporter that will provide timely and efficient coverage of the political campaigns.

Coverage of Political Campaigns

Coverage of political campaigns remains the most interesting part of political reporting in a diverse country like Nigeria. Campaign coverage takes the political correspondent to nooks and crannies of the country and the world at large. It exposes one to various towns, villages, communities, cultures, traditions and customs and the specific problems of development that confront each culture and people in the same country.

In some communities, the major problem is lack of good roads, in others, it is lack of potable water, while in some others, it is lack of health care. A political reporter on campaign tour is exposed to these issues. The campaign speeches and promises revolve around the Party manifesto. The political correspondent for the campaign team is expected to develop stories for his organization from the speeches, the requests that follow the speeches and most importantly, what the reporter saw, which the candidate and even the community may not have seen.

This is in addition to people and events that define the campaign, unforeseen developments and other side attractions. Except creativity and innovation are explored, campaign reports and speeches may become boring and marked with repetitions.

A political correspondent, especially for the electronic media, must watch out, remain professional, fair and balanced in all reports and in line with the electoral guidelines. While it is important to be close to the party, it is dangerous and unethical to assume political party membership in one's reports and approach to media coverage. A clear line between duty and association has to be drawn and carefully self-regulated and managed. It can be real fun when the reporter is attached to a popular candidate. With a popular candidate, the goodwill, personality and popularity of the candidate opens doors and make things easy for the reporter in any part of the country the campaign moves to.

However with a controversial, unpopular candidate, it can be quite risky if the campaign moves to resistant towns, villages and constituencies. In some cases, the resistance could result into conflicts, riots, and brutality capable of putting the lives of the campaign team at risk. Even with a popular candidate, the risks of accidents in the usual campaign convoys are real and frequent. I was part of the 12 political correspondents attached to MKO Abiola's 1993 presidential campaign team. We toured

Nigeria in and out. From Abakaliki to Argungu, Gwandu Emirate to Ilesha, Kaduna to Enugu, Sokoto to Port Hacourt, or Calabar to Dutse, Lagos to Kano, Maiduguri, Yobe, and Ilorin. We went everywhere.

MKO Abiola had a plane branded **Hope 93** that took us as a team with the candidate on board. Travelling with Abiola was real fun. With MKO, there was no boring moment once we were on board. His generosity and exceptional humour, oiled with rib- cracking proverbs, made the journey a delight. But two weeks into the national campaign tour, my Director in Lagos, Patrick Obazele, had left a message that I should get MKO Abiola to fly to Lagos to appear as the special guest on Radio Nigeria's popular programme, the *Radio Link*.

A similar directive had gone to my colleague, Gbenga Onayiga, to also get NRC Presidential Candidate, Bashir Tofa, on the same programme but on different dates so as to get a balance. The director said it was important for the presidential candidates to use the network programme to appraise the success of the campaign so far and to also answer questions directly from listeners on issues of the moment and on their campaign promises.

The task of getting MKO to interupt his campaign, which was at its peak at that time and was operated under a tightly managed, carefully drawn time-table, was like squeezing water out of rock. But with Chief Obazele, a reporter had no excuse to fail in any assignment. The pressure on me became unbearable when my colleague, Gbenga, who was regularly in touch, told me that he had already got Bashir Tofa to accept to be on the programme.

With the support of the MKO Campaign team and my colleagues on the beat, who were also looking for a reason to see their families in Lagos, MKO was pressured to accept to be on the programme. At that time, the campaign train was in Sokoto. I was thus asked to proceed to Lagos to make all arrangements before the arrival of the presidential candidate.

It is important to note here that as a political correspondent, you are in the best position to provide guidance and insights to your organization on how to host the politicians, the right language to use, the major issues that need to be discussed, the right questions to ask, the gaps in the campaign so far and indeed other relevant issues that would make the candidate appreciate and enjoy every time spent and accord your organization the deserved respect at the end of the day.

The only available flight on the Sokoto-Lagos route at that time was an airline called Hold Trade. It was this airline that I boarded back to Lagos. While on board, we ran into very severe turbulence. It was a horrifying experience. The turbulence was so much and as the Pilot was about to say something, possibly to calm the terrified passengers in what appeared to be a hopeless situation, the worst happened; the aircraft went almost 7ft down! There was dead silence in the aircraft as many passengers fainted. The earlier shouts of Allahu Akbar! Allahu Akbar! Jesus! Jesus!, gave way to dead silence. In all my years of traveling around the world, I had never encountered such scary turbulence. When the aircraft finally landed in Lagos, ambulances were waiting to evacuate those who had developed health problems arising from the turbulence on that flight. This is one hazard common in the coverage of campaigns. It was a horrible experience I always remember each time I board an aircraft for any trip, be it local or international.

Another important event occurred in my days as political correspondence in 1992 during the SDP National Assembly elections campaign tour of the country. I was also in the team of 12 political correspondents attached to the party's media corps. The team was led by the National Chairman, Babagana Kingibe and we travelled to various parts of the country. Again, after presenting the House of Representatives and Senatorial candidates in Sokoto at an impressive campaign rally on a Thursday, we all retired to Gigginya Hotel, located at the serene part of Sokoto, the state capital.

At that time, the hotel was very new, tastefully furnished and could possibly be rated as the best in Northern Nigeria. Before we were gracefully ushered into our rooms, the National Chairman addressed the media team for what he described as a job well done. "I am impressed with the media and publicity of all campaigns so far. Please keep it up," Alhaji Kingibe advised. "We are already one week into the campaign and it appears we need to have some rest here throughout this weekend as I move down to Maiduguri tomorrow morning to be with the family. I will join you guys and we hopefully shall continue with the journey on Monday morning. Please enjoy yourselves fully in this beautiful hotel and make sure you just help us sign the bills okay? Bye!" The national chairman left for Maiduguri.

For the purposes of the campaign, a major airline in Nigeria at that time, Okada Air, had designated a 20-seater aircraft each for the two political parties. The one designated to SDP was the one the chairman and the team were using. As soon as the chairman left, heaven was let loose. The rest of our colleagues boldly analyzed the Chairman's instruction to mean we were free to eat and drink anything that we wanted and just sign the bills because the party was buoyant and ready to pay. Some invited friends from town and parties began in most rooms.

At about evening that day, I had begun to feel feverish and had no reason to doubt that malaria attack was at hand. The fever later increased and was accompanied with severe headache, loss of appetite and vomiting. For the greater part of the recess, I was on medication, with the help of my colleague, the Radio Nigeria Correspondent in Sokoto, who procured some malaria tablets. I lamented the loss of the opportunity to participate in the free for all dining, wining, dancing and partying that characterized the recess, courtesy of the SDP Chairman's benevolence and open cheque. In fact, even the hotel staff at Gigginya Hotel, I learnt, became scared and wondered if the party would pay the bills that had been hugely accumulated.

Monday morning, as promised, the chairman was back. Unknown to all of us, the chairman had requested for the bills for our respective consumptions in the hotel. He painstakingly studied the bills and invited those whose bills were simply embarrassing to a conversation. Many were culprits. The consumptions included drinks that were even more than the reporters' monthly salary. I don't know what transpired between the chairman and each of those who faced the inquiry. However, I was invited too. But in my case, the chairman commended me for what he called a responsible bill. He advised me to keep it up. " My friend when people book you in a hotel and give you an open cheque to eat whatever you like and sign the bill, they simply want to know what kind of person you are, okay? You have a responsibility to respect yourself and ensure that you consume only those things that you can afford to put hands in your pocket and pay for easily, just in case your host chooses to question your bill. I am impressed that your bill was the most responsible. Please keep it up he commended. "Thank you Mr. Chairman," I answered. But if Baba had known that my bill was the lowest because I was sick and had no appetite, he would not have accorded me the underserved commendation. Nevertheless, I got the message loud and clear. That message was a big lesson for me personally even as I progressed in the profession. I took the message as an advice of a lifetime - don't abuse privileges. There is no free lunch anywhere. Every free gift requires decorum and responsibility. Unfortunately, in Nigeria, any free opportunity is an open invitation for abuse, greed, recklessness and impunity.

As reporters from developing countries such as Nigeria, we usually got fully-funded and sponsored invitations to political meetings and events. In some of these events, the hotels were fully paid for and we were free to make consumptions at the expense of our hosts. Many of us abused these privileges. When our hosts scrutinized the bill after we had gone, their discovery said a lot about our reputation. Even in open political events where we were expected to wine and dine with party bigwigs and leadership, we quite often scoop heaps of food in our plates and this often attracted the attention of other guests. The sad part is that most times, the heaps of food were left unconsumed while other guests who came after us for the buffet had no food to eat.

From my experience on the political beat, where such lunch and dinner offers are common, a political correspondent needs to find a way to match professional competence with integrity, decency, moral and ethical decorum. From my experience, personality has a lot to do with the source of the message and information.

The reporter must also be conscious of when the election begins and when it is expected to end, remain sensitive and strictly adhere to regulations and guidelines in line with the law.

Coverage of Elections

The conduct of an election under a democratic system is usually the responsibility of the electoral body set up for that purpose and not the media. In Nigeria, it is currently the duty of the Independent National Electoral Commission, INEC. At that time, it was called National

Electoral Commission with Prof Humphrey Nwosu as Chairman. Tonnie Iredia was Director, Public Affairs and responsible for media and public relations in the commission. He had the responsibility of managing and coordinating media coverage and reporting of election issues and activities, following the approved guidelines. Therefore, the reporter's job on the election day is highly regulated by the electoral guidelines which are usually full of Dos and Don'ts. The Reporter has the responsibility of studying these guidelines very carefully and understanding and internalizing them to avoid violation. These include the Electoral Act and the electoral timetable.

As I write this chapter, the INEC has, on Wednesday January 29th 2014, issued the timetable and schedule of activities for the 2015 general election in Nigeria. For a political correspondent, this is a fundamental development which needs to be clearly analyzed in a formal report. From the timetable, the specific dates for notice of election, commencement of campaign by political parties, collection of forms for all elections by political parties at INEC headquarters are now publicly known.

Also contained in the time-table are the dates for conduct of party primaries, deadline for submission of forms completed by candidates, including the specific days for the presidential, legislative, governorship and state houses of assembly elections. With this vital information released to the reporter and the public, the stage for planning for the coverage is set. The reporter's job in the implementation of the timetable is to cover, monitor and report with accuracy and balance how each and all of the activities are implemented by INEC, the response by the competing political parties, conflicts and their resolutions. In our days, the system was similar if not the same.

On each of the designated election days, the reporter's job is very sensitive. To carry out this function, the reporter requires an accreditation. The next stage is to monitor the voting process, collation of results and report the outcome based on certified information by the electoral body. This is followed by an in-depth analysis of matters arising from the exercise.

Chapter 6

Essentials in Legislative Reporting

The legislature is perhaps the most important arm of the three arms of government. This is in consideration of the fact that apart from the President and the Vice President, the majority of those high ranking officials who constitute the Executive and Judicial branches are either selected or appointed or both. But all legislators were directly elected by the people under the Presidential system in practise in Nigeria and directly represent the ordinary people.

The legislature therefore represents the custodian of citizens' interest and participation in any electoral system of a democratic society. In Nigeria, however, the legislature has not endured in culture and growth when compared with the other arms of government. The commonest reason

89

usually given for the poor performance of the legislature is that while the other two arms functioned effectively during military rule in Nigeria, the legislature at all levels were usually suspended along with the constitution each time the military intervened in the business of government of the nation. Being the one critical element that defines a democratic society, suspending the legislature usually signifies the total sucess of any military intervention.

Against this background, reporting the legislature by any broadcast media should be considered a serious business. These include coverage of the activities and legislative proceedings of the National and State Assemblies and even the legislative arms of the local governments at the grassroot.

I was exposed to the rudiments of legislative reporting in 1993 when I was deployed to Abuja to cover the Senate as part of the transition to civil rule programme of the Babangida Administration. I recall now that notable senators who were part of that Senate, whose tenure was cut short by the annulment of June 12, 1993 election include Senators Bola Ahmed Tinubu - Lagos, A.T Ahmed- Kogi, Albert Legogie – Edo, Liyel Imoke - Cross River, Emma Nwaka-Abia, Ebenezer Ikeyina- Anambra, among others. Senator Iyorchia Ayu of Benue State was elected Senate President with Albert Legogie as his deputy.

I also remember that Ms. Amal Pepple was the Clerk of the Senate while the Clerk of the National Assembly was Alhaji Adamu Fika. The importance of this background story is not to discuss all that happened or failed to happen during that period but to provide a basis to appreciate the job of a reporter posted to the National Assembly by a broadcast media. Although the period was brief, my experience in legislative reporting was later strengthened between 2001 and 2003 when I served the then President of the Senate, Anyim Pius Anyim as Special Adviser on Media and Public Relations. Thereafter, I became Radio Nigeria national political editor and head, network news political desk with National Assembly reporters under my supervision.

But back to 1993, the first challenges reporters faced were lack of knowledge, understanding and exposure to legislative proceedings, processes and methods, as many reporters were new to this aspect of journalism, after three decades of military rule. Besides, unlike now, there were very little or non-existent records and references to aid learning and human development. This informed the intervention of the then Director of United States Information Service, Mike O'Brien, whose office was based in Lagos, to use his position to mount a donor-funded training programme for National Assembly correspondents.

Officials of the United Nations Office in Lagos and the World Bank country office in Nigeria supported that training. A few Nigerians with experiences in the First Republic were equally part of the resource team. Those of us who were to form the core of the National Assembly press corps grabbed the opportunity of the training with two hands. For us, the training was a rare privilege and stepping stone.

The training exposed us to parliamentary procedures, the importance of plenary sessions, the committees and their relevance, methods of presentation and passage of bills, motions and resolutions. We were also exposed to such important issues like monitoring and oversight functions of the legislature and the role of the legislature in annual appropriations. Besides, we also studied the structure of the legislature, the leadership organs and their functions, the sitting arrangements in the chamber, the role of the majority party and the opposition, among others.

We were also told the need to identify each legislator with the party and constituency he or she represented in every of our reports no matter how often. We also learnt basic parliamentary ethics. This training was quickly followed by a similar one by the Nigerian Institute of Journalism, Ogba, Lagos in collaboration with a US-based institute. The outcomes of these trainings were productive and positive and reflected in the quality of the reports and analysis of issues emanating from the National Assembly during that short period. The importance of training and retraining of reporters on the legislative beat cannot be over-emphasized.

It is obvious from the above that, legislative reporting requires the reporter's in-depth understanding of the role of the National Assembly in a democracy and how this role impacts on law making, peace, security and development of society. It is also important to note the limits of powers of the National Assembly in relation to the powers and functions of the executive and judicial branches.

A legislative reporter also needs to know how bills become law; how bills originate and are presented through to first reading, referred to committees, second and third reading, as well as the importance of each of the stages in the life of a bill. What about the differences between President's bill and private member bill as well as the life span of a bill in a legislative calendar? A correspondent in the legislature also needs to know all the members of the chamber and their constituencies off-hand, including the role or position of the key players on important national issues.

When a broadcast journalist on the legislative beat presents reports, the difference is clear. But a legislative reporter with little knowledge of the issues and the structure of the parliament is simply an accident to the organization. The listener has a choice when such a reporter comes on air. From my experience, reporting the National Assembly requires these and more:

- Knowledge of the constituencies and the chamber structure.
- Knowledge of the principal officers.
- Knowledge of legislative procedure in the Senate and House of Representatives.
- Knowledge of the committees, their chairmen, respective roles and functions.
- Knowledge of important legislative aides and their influence, especially those responsible for media relations.

- Knowledge of the power play among the political parties that make up the chamber.

- Knowledge of important bills, their sponsors and contending interests.

- Knowledge of the position of each legislature or party caucus on bills and issues.

- In-depth knowledge of the Senate or House rules and legislative calendar.

- Understanding of the structure of the press corps and one's major competitors for stories.

- Reporter must follow strictly with ear- for- the news, the power dynamics in the National Assembly and events that unfold between the Assembly, the Executive and other arms.

- Knowledge of the role of "hangers-on" at the lobby and others who live on nothing else but rumour, blackmail and praise singing. They are always around the legislature no matter the security measures.

- Fairness, firmness, construction and professionalism in presentation of one's reports.

- The reporter must learn to identify each legislature with his/her constituency in every report.

- The reporter must avoid pestering legislators with all kinds of personal demands and requests.

- A reporter must carry his organization in high esteem.

As Special Adviser to the President of the Senate on Media Relations, I managed and related with the Senate press corps on the job on daily basis between the year 2000 and 2003. It was an important opportunity for robust professional engagement with reporters from over fifty media organisations directly attached to the Senate. I also had the responsibility of relating with editors, publishers within and outside the country on media issues surrounding Senate decisions in general and the President of the Senate in particular.

My background as a broadcaster and field reporter was quite helpful. It was a great opportunity for knowledge sharing and self-development. An important aspect that a legislative reporter should focus on is constant self-development and the ability to put in every effort to improve. Over the years, there have been great improvement in this area but more still needs to be done. If the reporter understands the issues, the procedure, the role of the principal officers and the structure and politics in the chamber, the work of reporting the legislature becomes real fun and eventful.

Chapter 7

Airport, Aviation and Business Matters

Aviation Beat

I covered the aviation industry as a reporter for the Federal Radio Corporation of Nigeria between 1991 and 1993. It was one of the three important beats in my kit as a young reporter. Upon resumption, I discovered that activities in the aviation sector in Nigeria then and even now, are dominated by the airlines, airport agencies and regulatory institutions, some of which were strategically located within the airport vicinity. They included the Ministry of Aviation, Federal Airport Authority of Nigeria, Federal Civil Aviation Authority, the National Air Space Management Agency, among others. There are also interested stakeholders and key players such as the industrial unions in the sector.

At the time I was a reporter, the Nigeria Airways, Okada Air, ADC Airline, Kabo, Chanchangi and a few others were the major national and private airlines that drove local air travel in Nigeria. They were also airlines whose operations were only limited to cargo. The international routes were dominated by British Caledonia, now British Airways, and many more. Nigeria was also a strong member of the International Air Transport Association (IATA), International Civil Aviation Organisation (ICAO), among other global reputable air travel administration and regulatory institutions. Our country also subscribed to several Bilateral Air Service Agreements (BASA). As I share this experience, some of the institutions are new while a few have been around for a while.

As a reporter deployed to cover airport and aviation, I arrived at the beat empty and ignorant of the structure of the aviation industry, how the airlines operated, the names, functions and role of navigational equipment such as the instrument landing system (ILs), Microwave landing system (MLs) and the more complex terminologies and their functions such as Very High Omni-directional radio range VoR., etc.

Others were air service agreements like Open, make-up of the runways, the airport terminals, the areas designated as the general aviation terminals - GAT, arrivals and departure halls, passenger and operational staff movements and restrictions in certain designated areas within the airport. I also needed to know about the work of such critical operational staff like the Air Traffic Controller.

Airport and aviation reporting was a technical beat, that required a great deal of knowledge, training and exposure. For instance, understanding revenue generation streams in the aviation industry was also a huge challenge. These included the role of travel agencies, connections with the airlines and the airport management in terms of certification, regulation and revenue remittances, computation, determination and issuance of landing and parking permits for the aircraft by the airlines. These and more important issues are what a reporter in the beat needs to know before such a reporter, especially for the broadcast media, will be in a position to inform, educate, and enlighten the public about people and events in the industry. This is one major problem a reporter posted to a beat must face. Understanding the industry, the business environment and the contemporary policies that drive the conduct of business in the industry is a critical success factor that a reporter, especially for the broadcast media, cannot ignore. The quality of a report from a reporter who understands the industry and one who does not, shows clearly in the content and delivery of the message on radio.

At the aviation beat at the Murtala Muhammed Airport, I was opportuned to have met one Lateef Lawal of the Tribune Newspapers, who as at 1991, had spent over 15 years reporting aviation. I quickly made friends with Lateef, Titus Agbo of the Democrat, Abu Jimoh of Triumph, Ukpong and Isiaka Aliagon of the Guardian, Obuke and Davies of the Daily Times, and Deola Fadairo who, at the time, was Chair, League of Airport and Aviation

Correspondents. I had no other choice than to immediately embrace the rigorous learning exercise if I must report and discuss aviation effectively.

These efforts were also further enhanced by series of trainings that organisations, institutions and industry unions in the sector deliberately at the time exposed reporters to, all in the bid to encourage in-depth knowledge of the sector. At that time, the Nigerian College of Aviation Technology, Zaria effectively supported airport and aviation reporting with series of trainings. That was between 1990 and 1992. The airlines too helped with series of exposure flights to interesting destinations.

One of the direct and reliable sources of information for any media organization is the aviation beat. Airports were a gold mine of information and news beyond the core operation and activities of airports. At major airports, the aviation correspondents have the responsibility to "block" very influential public official at the center of public policies and controversies to provide explanations, clarify issues, make pronouncements, and give powerful statements that deepen public understanding, debate and discussions on contemporary and burning national issues. This is because the airport is one sure route the Presidents, Governors, Legislators, Ministers and most news makers in the society use for travels. These news makers hardly use any other route.

And since access to these individuals in the office environments is fraught with difficult and man-made obstacles, the aviation beat is where the reporter has to lay ambush. Most serious editors depend on the aviation reporter for headlines especially on "a dry day". But unfortunately, apart from Lagos, where airport/aviation reporters have a strong base under the aegis of League of Airport and Aviation Correspondents, there is no presence of airport correspondents at the Nnamdi Azikiwe International Airport Abuja in spite of the incredible traffic of personalities and news makers that fly in and out of the Federal Capital City on daily basis. This is a huge gap in information source that has not been addressed.

I recall that around 1991 and unknown to many Nigerians, the Federal Government, under the Ibrahim Babangida administration, had commenced quiet but sustained discussions with the Israeli Government on possible restoration of diplomatic relations between Nigeria and Israel. At that time, General Ike Nwachukwu was Nigeria's Foreign Minister. Relations between the two countries, I learnt, had broken down about and during the Nigerian Civil war.

As airport and aviation correspondent, one night, just before 10pm, I had dozed off at the Airport Press Centre while waiting for the complex Lagos traffic to ease out before leaving for home, after every other reporter had left for home. I was woken by loud movements of people around the Airport Protocol Lounge where the Press Centre was located. As I opened my eyes, I saw Gen Ike Nwachukwu arriving from God knows which country.

While the protocol officers and security men struggled to usher him into the lounge, I headed quickly to the

101

General with my recorders to find out where he was coming from and the purpose of his visit. "Good evening General," I greeted. "How are you?" he answered in a polished deep tone that reflected fatigue of one coming home after a long journey. "I am fine, your Excellency, where are you coming from," I quickly asked in the midst of struggling and pushing for space and attention among his security men and overzealous aides who perhaps viewed the sudden appearance of a press man that late evening as an attempt to disturb their work . "Please allow him!" the General ordered. "I have just arrived from Israel," General Nwachukwu continued." You may not be aware of this, but we have commenced discussions with Israel on possible restoration of diplomatic ties which, as you know, was broken unfortunately during the civil war. So the Federal Government thinks it is time we look at the issues again with a view to seeking ways and means of rebuilding the relations in the interest of the citizens, government and business between the two countries," the Foreign Minister explained. "And how are the discussions going," I chipped in quickly. "Very well, from our series of meetings so far, I am convinced that the two countries are keen and committed to normalizing relations within the shortest possible time, thank you very much." General Nwachukwu concluded and headed straight to his car which had now been positioned at the main entrance of the Lagos Airport Presidential Lounge. The interview ended at 18 minutes before 10 p.m. I immediately rushed to the Press Centre and in few minutes, my story was ready:

Nigeria and Israel have commenced talks to restore diplomatic relations between the countries. The Minister of Foreign Affairs, General Ike Nwachukwu, announced this in Lagos while speaking with Airport Correspondents last night, shortly on arrival from Israel.

The Minister explained that although diplomatic relations between Nigeria and Israel was broken during the civil war, the time has come to re-examine the issues. General Ike Nwachukwu stressed that the two countries believed that normalizing relations will be in the best interest of their governments, business and citizens of the two countries. Radio Nigeria Aviation Correspondent, Orji Ogbonnaya Orji, reports that no deadline was given by the Minister for conclusion of the talks and restoration of the diplomatic relations.

The story was faxed immediately to the Broadcasting House Ikoyi and it was number one headline at the 10 p.m bulletin that night. I felt proud that I broke that news to Nigeria. At that time, most, if not all, print and electronic media organizations in Nigeria not only listen to, but monitor, record and later transcribe all FRCN (Radio Nigeria) major news broadcasts for use as stories in their own respective organizations. The following day, which was a Monday, the story was in all major Nigeria national dailies, including the Daily Times. I learnt from the media

103

team of the Foreign Ministry that Gen. Nwachukwu was quite happy that by speaking with just one reporter he met at the airport, the story was all over the country.

While I received accolades from here and there, all my colleagues in the aviation beat were queried by their respective editors for missing such a big story. This put me on a collision course with the leadership and members of League of Airport and Aviation Correspondents, who argued that the way I drafted my story gave the impression that the Foreign Minister addressed a scheduled Press Conference at the Airport and they were deliberately absent from the assignment.

The league, which still remains the professional group that regulates aviation reporting, drew my attention to where I wrote that: "The Minister of Foreign Affairs, General Ike Nwachukwu announced this in Lagos while speaking with Airport Correspondents last night, shortly on arrival from Israel."

The point, my colleagues maintained, was that my story should have been attributed to Radio Nigeria Aviation Correspondent because the interview in question was exclusive to me and only I attended and conducted the interview. I was off the hook with a fine but more importantly, a lesson. And the lesson for all of us was that the Aviation Beat is one beat where a story can break at any time. The aviation reporter is on duty and at alert all round the clock. There is no resuming or closing time. This is partly because aviation matters are global and highly unpredictable. For instance, the aviation reporter is expected to be at the airport waiting for a VIP passenger without having information on the VIP's travel plans, arrival and departure time, objective of the trip and if the VIP will be willing to speak on either arrival or departure. But the aviation reporter has to be there on standby for sudden arrival and departure of VIPs, news makers and other politically inclined persons and personalities whose views shape and shake people and events in society. The same goes for air crashes, accidents and mishaps which may occur and when they do, a reporter that misses it may have to look for another job because no editor is prepared to accept excuses for such lapses.

Reporting aviation therefore taught me some lessons about truancy, lateness to duty, lousiness, laxity and poor attention to assigned duties. I also learnt that a reporter has a responsibility to study an assigned beat very well no matter how technical in nature such a beat is.

Reporting Business and Finance Matters

A reporter on this beat, especially from the broadcast media, is faced with the challenge of breaking down financial, economic and business terminologies to enhance the knowledge and understanding of listeners and viewers, most of whom are rural dwellers. For instance, a finance and business reporter must understand the various dynamics and dimensions of a country's economy and how this affects the society we live in. He has to learn about trade imports and exports and finance and how they connect with public policy and ultimately, the people's well-being.

The reporter should adequately understand such development issues which influence economic policies such as insufficient jobs and poverty, domestic and foreign debts, food security, housing, education, etc. In the capital market, I am aware that only but a few shareholders who attend annual general meetings of banks, companies and other investment institutions understand and follow issues when the financial annual reports on the performance of their companies are being presented. And if the shareholders who have invested their funds in the companies do not know these things, of what interest will media reports be to the listeners who have no equity interest or attachment?

The reality is that many people who buy shares in most companies hardly attend meetings but wait for media reports to tell them how their companies have performed during the period under review. But do our reports make meaning to the listeners such that they are in a position to access the companies? The job and responsibility of the business reporter thus become important.

There is need for the business and financial reporter to develop interest in these and other issues required to inform and educate the listeners. These include financial analysis of interest rates, inflation, foreign and domestic debts, annual budgets and other economic issues that influence the people's purchasing power and living standards. Others are reports and financial statements of banks, economic aggregates related to growth and development and other allied matters for which people often depend on the Business and Finance Correspondent in order to appreciate and understand.

To be able to develop stories and tackle issues that educate, enlighten and inform the audience effectively through fair, objective, accurate and balanced reporting, the correspondent must bear in mind, while developing stories along these issues, that the listeners have a choice and right to tune to another station once the information does not make any sense to him. One sure way to perform well as a reporter in this area is to carefully understand the industry and develop simple strategies to drive the message home. A business and finance reporter for the broadcast media must learn to break down information and data contained in the report of banks' annual financial statements and balance sheet for basic radio message and statements. A reporter misses the point when we begin to hear such complex terminologies as "the total equity holding of the bank stood at so so and so billions of naira" and he is very likely to lose many of his listeners. What is equity holding? We need to explain. The same applies to stock market analysis on radio and television by business and financial correspondents. Business and finance jargons such as "values of equity declined or improved", "market capitalization went down or up", "all share index depreciated or appreciated" and so on, remain quite complex for the listeners and difficult to understand and frustrating. For the print media, the reader may find time to consult the dictionary but in the case of radio/TV audience, the message is transient and needs to be broken down. I do not share the view that stock market and certain business and financial issues are for the exclusive preserve of a privileged few in society.

I have observed that the difference between developed, developing and under-developed society is the amount of information available to the citizens. I do think that our people's very poor knowledge and understanding of budget issues, opportunities in the stock market and trade and investment potential in Nigeria is a function of lack of information. Thus, the business and financial reporter in the broadcast media which are the nearest, fastest and most affordable media to the people, have the enormous responsibility to break down the message for easy grassroot understanding.

To be able to carry out this function, the correspondents in this beat require time and interest to know the beat very well, the key players, the business language and then help the audience by making the language of presentation simple and friendly to the listeners.

Orji as a young reporter in 1990

Presenting a live programme in the studios

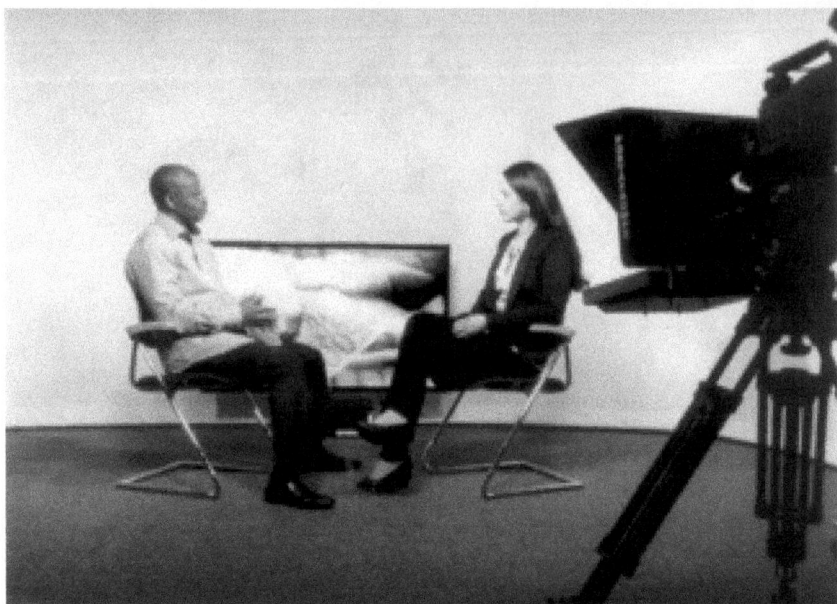

As a guest on an interview programme at the studios of
Deutsche Welle Television, Bonn, Germany

On a study tour of the Legislature State of Maryland,
Annapolis, USA

With some classmates at the Harvard Kennedy School, Cambridge, Massachusettes (2008)

With media practitioners while on training at the GIZ Institute for International Cooperation, BadHonnef, Germany

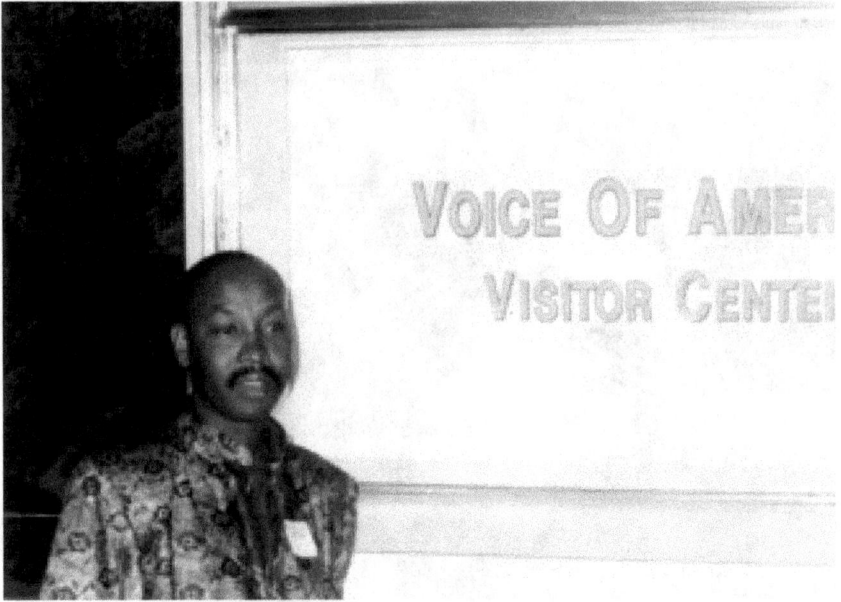

On training at the Voice of America

At the Harvard Square, Cambridge, Massachusettes, in 2008
covering the public protest of citizens from Tibet region

On a study tour of the United State's Congress

On arrival in Sydney, Australia for a conference

From left: Chief Joop Berkhout, Chukwuma Soludo, Hakeem
Bello Osagie, Orji, and El-Rufai at an event

Chapter 8

Coverage of Ceremonies (Weddings, Birthdays and Burials)

L istening to reports and watching coverage of ceremonies such as high society weddings, birthdays and anniversaries can be uninteresting, sad and frustrating when the broadcast reporter fails to understand the importance of conveying the excitement, happiness and glamour that usually come with such occasions. Accurate and proper reporting is possible through creative, incisive and in-depth description of the environment, people, events and attractions that define such ceremonies. However, the reporter will be unable to do that if there is no capacity to interpret the event. Interpretation of the event requires defining what the occasion means to the organizer and what that has to do with public interest, the objective of the occasion, possible impact and lessons.

Interpretation of the event also requires a clear understanding of how the coverage of the event will align with the news of the day in the organization and the expectations of the editor in terms of news content when the reporter comes back with the story.

To do this effectively, the reporter must ask himself or herself the following questions:

- Why am I at this event and what is the interest of my media organization in this coverage?

- Why is this ceremony different from others?

- What features make the occasion unique?

- Who among the organizers and invited guests will speak eloquently and capture the essence of the event?

- How many short interviews do I need to complement my story?

- At what point will I be done with the coverage?

- How do I present the story to attract attention and meaning?

A reporter sent to cover big celebration ceremonies has the responsibility of captivating the attention of the audience through creative introduction of the story. The introduction of the story must be appealing; ranging from perhaps the music, exchange of pleasantries, speeches or even an unusual side attraction with humour that captures the attention of the listener exclusively. Such reports are usually better with creative introduction. However, there are no rigid rules but one has to have creativity, innovation and style flexibility. In the main report, the listener is entitled to a brief background to the event, the justification for the celebration, the preparation, cost implication and the linkage with individuals, group or public interest if any.

It is also important to invite the listener into the world of glamour, opulence and style that puts the event ahead of others in recent times. Equally important is a comment on the attendance of the high and mighty as well as the connection with the personality, wealth, power, influence and position of the host in the society. When our reports are benchmarked with these and more details, the listener will have something to take away. Unfortunately, I find most ceremony media reports lacking in these ingredients, leaving the listener in the cold and sometimes, frustrated.

Coverage and Reporting of Weddings

They are several reasons why the media would be interested in weddings. The first reason may be that of opulence, affluence and an attempt to display wealth and money by the celebrant. This is common among weddings involving children of rich and influential public officers. This kind of media coverage has little or no news value except for show of wealth. But it can be of news value if either the bride or bridegroom is very poor and of an unusual background. Like having a mechanic marry the Governor's daughter for instance. This is an unusual occurrence in

Nigeria and will therefore attract public interest and hence, the media.

My introduction to this type of story can take this form:

Archibong David, a highway motor-mechanic recently landed a goldmine when one of the convoys in a Governor's entourage broke down.

The incident occured on Shagamu-Benin-Ore road, as Governor X was on his way to an unknown destination. While the convoy was on the move, one of the cars in the long convoy suddenly broke down, thereby forcing the convoy, including the Governor, to stop. It was at that point that Archibong David, the roadside mechanic, rushed to the scene and offered to assist."

Cue in: (voice of Archibong David, the mechanic, explaining why he went to the scene and what he did.

Cue out: (end of the voice of Archibong after his narration)

The dexterity, efficiency and commitment with which Archibong David, the roadside mechanic, fixed the car in record time, earned him an invitation from the governor to the Government House. At the Government House, Archibong was offered a job as mechanic to handle many vehicles that had broken down and whose repairs had seem imposible fo other mechanics. In his new sojourn as government house mechanic, Archibong David shifted his attention from broken down vehicles and went after the Governor's daughter. His efforts yielded dividend recently when the Governor's daughter, Roseline X, asked for the mechanic's hand in marriage.

Cue in: (voice of Archibong David narrating how he met the Governor's daughter)

Cue out: (end of Archibong's story)

A state wedding for the couple was held at the Gracious Cathedral in the state capital. And the roll call of dignitaries was endless; Governor X, other governors, ministers, legislators, industrialists, business associates of the Governor, etc. It was easier to count the high and mighty in the country that did not come than to identify those that attended.

Cue in: (The governor's daughter, Roseline, explaining the choice of a mechanic as husband in spite of her opulent background.)

Cue out:(End of her story.)

The Governor equally explained why he supported his daughter's choice of a mechanic son-in-law.

Cue in: (Governor's narration.)

Cue out:(End of the Governor's interview.)

113

The joy of David Archibong's parents was unlimited.

Cue in:(The parents express their views.)

Cue out: (End of parents' speech.)

We also sampled the views of other dignitaries at the event.

Cue in:(Vox pop interviews on the event.)

Cue out: (End of vox pop.)

Concluding statements- End of report.

Other kinds of weddings include mass weddings for the old and aged, when a physically challenged lady marries an able-bodied man or vice versa or a man with over 50 wives getting set for another wedding as was recorded recently in Minna, Niger State. Under these and more peculiar situations, the reporter has to follow the coverage and narrate the story from the following perspectives:

- Point of preparations
- The reasons behind the union (from the two parties)
- The parents', or guardian's, opinion
- Are there any legal or customary violations?
- The sermon or advice at the wedding
- Atmosphere at the event, including attendance and side attractions
- The implication of the union to the community

Reporting Birthdays and Similar Occasions

Birthday ceremonies coverage requires similar but slightly different approach. This is because many talk publicly about their birthdays, receive accolades and birthday wishes but hardly celebrate them. Only few mark their birthdays with parties and loud celebrations and this is rare, especially among men. Women, however, more often than men, celebrate their birthdays, especially young ladies, who often use birthdays to extort money from their lovers and admirers. Many single ladies who celebrate their birthdays often do so on the bill of many prospective suitors and lovers and hardly on theirs.

However, birthdays that have become quite common include fiftieth or seventieth birthday. In Nigeria, with high mortality rate, it is quite expected that this is a landmark worthy of celebration. Nevertheless, celebration is only called for if those years were punctuated with visible measurable achievements. It is these achievements, among others, that must engage the attention of the reporter. Below are the angles which the coverages must focus on:

- When was the celebrant born?
- Background to the birth profile.
- Were there challenges while growing up, and is any of them of public interest?
- How did the celebrant overcome them?
- What are the celebrant's achievements in life and their connection with public good?

- Details of the celebration; the attendance, the glamour and the opulence.

- What are the things that will change from that moment onwards?

The reporter armed with these and more facts has enough information to write a story and drive the message home with humour, excitement and joy.

Coverage of Burial Ceremonies

Life is but a walking shadow, a poor player that struts and frets his hour upon the stage and then is heard no more: it is a tale told by an idiot, full of sound and fury, signifying nothing.

William Shakespeare(Macbeth).

These immortal words of Shakespeare are a reminder that death is an end that will come when it will come. When this happens, it is expected to be reported in the media if the deceased or the circumstances surrounding the death are news worthy. As we are aware, it is not every death that attracts media attention. Media coverage of burial ceremonies are determined and defined by personality, service and circumstances.

Reporting burials for the broadcast media is one area where we have a huge gap, probably because these events are not as glamorous as weddings and high society birthdays. But of course if the burial is that of a stalwart like Nelson Mandela, as happened recently, we find that

116

there can be no bigger story that day anywhere, at home or abroad. However, most of the reports on radio and television do very little or nothing to convey the emotions of pain, sorrow, hopelessness, anger and frustration that death represents. Most of the reports we hear on radio and watch on television focus more on the so-called important dignitaries that attended the burial; ignoring the more important information about the background of the deceased, why he/she died, health challenges leading to death, if the death could have been avoided, service to humanity and the fate of those left behind. I also find it unprofessional to have reports on burials and deaths presented in a voice and tone that conveys no emotion, sense of loss and sympathy.

What I find common is that reports on deaths and burials are presented with the normal voice and tone used for other non-emotional news items. This is very wrong.

Ideally, a report on a burial for the broadcast media should begin with a creative description of the atmosphere at the mortuary, the casket, the ambulances and the motorcade to the venue where the funeral ceremonies would hold. This should gradually progress to the situation in the family, the wife, children and relatives' responses to the arrival of the corpse. The reporter also needs to take the audience directly into the church service and cover the most important messages contained in the sermon, the funeral orations, tributes and the atmosphere at the grave side. Creative description of each of these scenes in an emotion laden voice that clearly reflects concern, compassion, pity and sorrow are desirable. During my career, I had the opportunity of covering State burials of a former Head of State and a former King/President respectively. Each of the two presidential burials came under different circumstances.

The first was the burial of Nigeria's former Head of State, General Sani Abacha, in Kano on June 8, 1998. I covered the event from the Presidential Villa through the Abuja airport ceremonies, service at the Kano central Mosque, until his corpse was lowered to the grave with full military honors in his country home, GRA, Kano. The report of that burial was by my estimation one of my best in terms of description and delivery. It was graphic, historical, informative, and emotional at the same time, making bold statements about life and vanity of human desires.

The day Abacha died makes compelling reading and is one of the most engaging chapters in my first book, **Inside Aso Rock**, a Spectrum Books, Ibadan publication which is available online at - www.spectrumbooksonline.com.

Another Presidential burial that I attended and covered for the Radio Nigeria Network Service was that of King Hussein of Jordan. King Hussein was not just one of the most popular and influential Kings in the Middle East but the President and ruler of Jordan who reigned and ruled Jordan for over 50 years. Besides, King Hussein was seen as one of the major stabilizing factors in the Israeli-Palestinian/Arab conflict as a result of his neutrality and mediation role at the time. His death and burial was therefore a major international news event from every angle.

However, while in Jordan as a reporter, I constantly reminded myself that in spite of the political and diplomatic nature of the event, the fact remained, as Wole Soyinka wrote, that "the man died" and the event is a burial ceremony. As a result, grief, sympathy and a sense of loss associated with death and burial must influence the report.

I recall the introduction to that report:

> *Tears flowed freely from both sides in the Israeli- Palestinian Conflict as the body of the man at the center of the peace negotiation, King Hussein of Jordan, was buried.*
>
> *State House Correspondent, Orji Ogbonnaya Orji, on the line from Amman Jordan, reports that the burial was more emotional than political.*
>
> *Men, women and children with faces full of grief, lined up the streets here in Aman, the Jordan capital, to catch a glimpse of the body of a man, pay tribute to a king, who many acknowledged made more than enough sacrifices to ensuring development in his country, peace and security in the Middle East (and my report continued...)*

I recently followed on CNN, the live coverage of the burial of Nelson Mandela on December 15, 2013. Of greater interest to me in that coverage was the emotions and grief shown by South Africans as they lined up to pay tribute to the body of Mandela while lying in state at the union building in Pretoria.

As a reporter who was present on May 10, 1994 at the swearing-in of Nelson Mandela as the first black President of that country in the same union building in Pretoria, I wept as I tried to reconcile the relief, sense of freedom from bondage, excitement and joy on the faces of black South Africans at the event, and their pain and grief over the death of the same in whom they found liberation and freedom.

My eyes were glued to the CNN during the coverage of church service in Mandela's hometown, Gunu, as I watched the emotional commentary that described every moment, the essence of holding the service in Mandela's village, the basis for the choice of each of the hymns sang during the service, how the officiating priests were selected and how each of these decisions related with Nelson Mandela's sojourn on earth. The description of the event contained such details as who qualified to attend the service and their connection with Nelson Mandela and his immediate family.

The high point of the coverage to me was at the graveside. The camera and the commentator were simply terrific as they brought the world's attention to the burial site, following the movement of the corpse in a military ambulance from the church through the valleys and hills to the graveside. At the graveside, I saw the futility or vanity of divorce, separation and marital conflict when Winnie and Gracia were the only women at Mandela's graveside. I asked myself: if Mandela should wake up and see Winnie by his graveside, how would he feel? Would it be forgiveness that she could stand by him at this last moment despite their differences? Or anger? I also waited to see the most emotional and perhaps traumatic part of the burial between Winnie and Gracia. Who will the South African President hand over the South African Flag as a baton in the race to carry on the Mandela legacy? The CNN cited family instruction as reason to deny millions of viewers around the world the opportunity to view that aspect as well as the climax, when Nelson Mandela's body was lowered to the grave. These are the kinds of emotions and questions which efficient coverage and reporting of burials can provoke in the minds of listeners or audiences if the broadcast reporter is sensitive to the peculiar nature of this assignment.

Chapter 9

Tips in Conducting Interviews and Editorial Writing

A good friend in the legal profession, Deji, once told me an amusing story of how he sat in his chamber, praying for a potential client to engage him with a big case. "As I sat wondering where and how this could happen," he narrated, "my doors flung open and a man ran into my chamber, shouting, "lawyer please help me, they have taken me to court. I swear! I did not do anything." My friend said he looked at the man in anger and asked him to get up. Then I promptly informed him that, "this office, this chamber, was set up for those who have done something! And since you have not done anything, please quietly leave my office now."

My friend's encounter explains vividly the need for interviews in broadcasting, either for radio or television.

The condition is no different for the print media. Interviews are for those who have something to say, something to contribute, and those who are doing or have done something. Interviews also become topical and interesting with someone who has information to share, someone in a position to know and someone whose views will be taken seriously on important national issues of public interest. The opposite example to illustrate this here is the experience of a senior reporter at NTA Lagos in the second republic, narrated to me by close friend and colleague. The then President of the Senate, Dr Joseph Wayas, had had a major disagreement with the Speaker of the House of Representatives, the late Chief Edwin Ume-Ezeoke. Having interviewed the Speaker, the NTA team arrived at Dr Wayas' Marina, Lagos, official residence, and with his consent set up their gear-camera, lighting and all. Dr Wayas appeared in his full *agbada* robe, sat down in front of the camera and the NTA man fired the question: "Mr. President, can you tell our viewers what is really the cause of dispute between you and the Speaker of the House? To the shock and utter consternation of the NTA crew, Dr Wayas looked straight into the camera and uttered just four words: "No comment! No comment!" After all this preparation and expectation! Well, here is the lesson. A reporter should never speak to someone who has nothing to say or does not want to say something. It is like the man who has done nothing wrong coming to a laywer.

In this category of those who may not want to say anything, even if they can, are public sector executives in sensitive positions whose actions and inactions affect the public. Others are politicians, legislators, private sector executives, media chiefs and civil society activists. Furthermore, others who fall into this special category are those at the center of one form of controversy or another, champions or opponents of issues of public interest, etc. If these and other basic requirements are in place by the producer's estimation, choice of resource person for the interview may be weighed on the scale of the following critical success factors.

- In-depth knowledge of the subject matter.

- Fluency and eloquence.

- Ability to drive home points with clarity, proof and examples.

- Tolerance of other views.

- Civility and politeness in responding to questions.

For the broadcast anchor, moderator and producer of the programme, the following factors are critical:

- Rich contact data base.

- Adequate preparation for the interview.

- The studios, studio consumables and operational staff need to be ready and on stand-by.

- Guest should not be kept waiting on arrival at the broadcasting house. It is discourteous for someone who has honored your invitation at the expense of other schedules to be treated this way.

- Good understanding of the subject matter through reading and deliberate research on available information and data.

- Good questions should be carefully developed and outlined in sequence.

- The interview should begin with a well-researched introduction of the issue and why the guest is invited.

- In the introduction of the issue, briefly speak about the guest and why the guest is suitable and qualified to speak on the subject.

- There is also the need to develop the ability to ask follow up questions, based on the issues raised by the guest.

- Follow up questions can only be possible if the moderator, interviewer or producer is listening attentively and following the explanations of the guest while the interview session is in progress. We have some interviewers who sleep off due to the chilling air condition in the studios, leaving the guest to be "a loose cannon shooting in all directions without control". This is terrible and is exactly what an interview should not be.

Do not begin by asking the guest to introduce himself or the subject. This is a common mistake and does not present the interviewer as someone who is prepared or did adequate research.

- Ability to ask informed follow-up questions through polite interjections at intervals in the course of the interview is very important; this shows the guest that the reporter also understands the issues very well. It is also important to always bring the guest back to the topic under discussion in cases of digression.

- The interviewer, moderator and producer must be neat, smartly dressed and good looking. How can your esteemed guest come into the studio well-dressed and reflecting his or her corporate standing in society and the host, moderator and producer welcoming the guest are shabbily dressed with body odor? This instantly lowers the morale of the interview and gives the guest a bad impression about your media house.

- Lastly, never argue with your guest or show off your knowledge on an issue. Remember the public wants to listen to your guest, not you.

I am a loyal audience of Channels TV's early morning current affairs programme - Sunrise Daily, anchored by two young men and a lady - Maope, Sulaiman and Chamberlain. The concept of the programme is not just good but very good. The presenters or moderators are equally good and quite knowledgeable on the issues. The programme is excellent in the choice of quality of guests.

They always bring on board, "people who have done something, people who are doing something and people who have something to say" everytime I have watched. Besides, the programme always features important topical issues of public interest . These, to me, are basic conditions for interview.

However, my problem with the presenters of this programme is that they have a tradition of engaging their guests, the resource persons they have labored to bring on the programme, in unnecessary arguments. The team hardly allows the guests the freedom to state their case. They argue and interrupt their guests, making it difficult for the guests to conclude their explanations. Their guests often battle for the opportunity to drive home their points. This, to me, is wrong and needs to be stopped. When we argue with our guests, we make them forget important issues they want to explain, or clarify.

I can cite two examples in this regards. On January 28th, 2014, the National Chairman of Labour Party, Dan Nwanyanwu, was on this programme. His mission, among others I guess, was possibly to state his party's position on the current national issue of discourse – a directive by All Progressive Congress – (APC) to block all executive bills in the National Assembly, including the 2014 Appropriation Bill and National Assembly clearance of service chiefs recently appointed by President Jonathan.

The consequences of that directive to the public and the public reactions that followed the directive made it topical. Frequent interruptions and engagement of the chairman in arguments adversely affected what could have been a very great programme. This was also the scenario on the following day, January 29th, 2014, when Tunde Fasakin of the All Progressive Congress came on the same programe to apparently respond to Labour Party's position and state the case of his party. These studies are simply to draw attention to mistakes we should avoid while conducting interviews, especially for the broadcast media. It is in no way an attempt to assess Channels TV for the wonderful job the station is doing in the industry. This focus on Channels TV is because they are doing something that no one can ignore.

Beyond these observations, I confess that I am one of the loyal audiences of Channels Television in Nigeria. My major attractions to the station are many. One of them is Channels TV News at 10pm. I hardly miss the news because I think they clearly strive to present the news with constructive content, they put a lot of efforts into balance and depth and they widen the audiences' perspectives by bringing in suitable resource persons to clarify, explain and educate.

Besides, the stations' news presenters are just good; their measured pace on the bulletin, voice talent, comportment and confidence on the screen are excellent. But what I admire most in all of these is the authority and sense of seriousness and urgency with which the presenters hold the attention of their audience. Nevertheless, there is room for improvement in both news and programmes concept, content, variety and presentation.

Back on the need for one to understand the issues at hand during interviews, I was one of the guests at the 2013 World Anti-Corruption Day celebrated in Abuja at the Shehu Musa Yar'adua Conference Centre . The World Anti-Corruption Day was organized by the Federal Government's Technical Unit on Governance and Anti-corruption to draw national and international attention to the dangers of corruption in national development, policy measures in place to combat corruption in Nigeria and how these efforts have worked or failed to work.

A group of journalists from the print and electronic media sent a message to me that they wanted to interview Zainab Ahmed, the Executive Secretary of Nigeria Extractive Industries Transparency Initiative, NEITI (an anti-corruption agency in the oil and gas sector under the Presidency). I currently work in NEITI as the Agency's Director, Communications. At their request, I discussed with the Executive Secretary and secured the time for the interview.

The journalists arrived on the specific date and time and were promptly ushered in for the exercise. After my preamble on the mission of the journalists and the need for the interaction, I declared the session open for questions. I was shocked that the first person did not get the name of the organization right and the question asked was unrelated to the work of NEITI. I quickly cut in to make some corrections and provide links to put him on the right track, but the intervention didn't help because basic knowledge of the issues was clearly lacking.

The other three journalists that attempted to come to the rescue were even worse, as their own mistakes demonstrated evident lack of education on the subject matter which, as the saying goes, is more dangerous than ignorance. I suspended the interview, pleaded for the understanding of the Executive Secretary, took some time out quickly, drafted the likely questions that would be of interest to NEITI and passed them to each of them. It wasn't until then that some progress was made.

But there were no follow-up questions because an in-depth knowledge of the issues were lacking. After the encounter, I assembled these colleagues in my office, had an educative session with them which they all appreciated. I also informed them that a book was in the offing to save others from similar mistakes.

In my career in broadcasting, I loved interviewing and have been part of many high level interviews. Apart from interviews on assignments and at press conferences in several beats I have covered, including the State House and the Presidential Villa, I have also been invited to participate as a member of panel of senior journalists on the Presidential Media Chat. That was in one of the sessions during the Obasanjo administration.

The Presidential Media Chat is a live national radio and television programme where high ranking journalists take on a sitting President of Nigeria on the policies of his administration and other key national issues. Indeed, Media Chat was television's answer to *The President Explains*, a monthly Presidential Talk Show which Radio Nigeria introduced with President Obasanjo in 2002 when Eddie

Iroh was Director General. But my real exposure to the rudiments of conducting interviews came handy when I was presiding over a Radio Nigeria popular current affairs programme, Eagle Square.

With all modesty, Eagle Square was my baby on Radio Nigeria network service. It was conceived and developed as an independent, courageous and insightful programme on governance, transparency and accountability, strictly for public officers and other news makers who have "done something"; the programme was not for "those who have not done anything."

It was against this background that my guests on Eagle Square were carefully chosen. Looking back, I recall that my first guest on the programme was Obiageli Ezekwesili in early 2004. At that time, she had just joined the Obasanjo Administration's economic reform team and was heading a unit in the Presidential Villa called Budget Monitoring and Price Intelligence Unit.

The only information available to the public was that there was one very tough, no-nonsense woman hired in the Villa by President Obasanjo, specifically to scrutinize the cost of all contracts and that without the signature of this very powerful woman, no project could be implemented. Another unverified rumor was that it was perhaps easier to go to heaven, dine and wine with the angels than to see the woman.

These rumours and misinformation were all over and got stronger at a time I was desperately searching for an influential personality who has done or is doing something remarkable to use to launch the programme. And this woman, from all I heard about her, met the criteria. Again, she was just new and relatively unknown to the media in Nigeria with respect to her new job and new position. Her job was so important, yet the public had no information on the objective, principles, methods of operation and expected impacts and benefits to society.

I thought she was well-suited for this programme which would afford her the opportunity to explain her side and her work. From my wide contacts and consultations, I got through to Oby Ezekwesili on telephone. I was humbled by her courtesy on phone without undue protocol. After exchange of pleasantries, I immediately put through my request for her to be my first guest on the programme. She gave me time to explain what the new programme was set to achieve, the reach and the audience. I told her of the need to explain her work to reduce the rumour, misinformation, misconception and propaganda that was all over. "Sure, I will! Can you hold on a minute, let me look at my schedule?" she requested. And I did. That was it.

She kept her word; she was on the programme on the scheduled date and exactly on time. The interview was long, elaborate, detailed and quite engaging, informative and interesting. Her explanations were incisive, expository, educative and eloquent. Obiageli Ezekwesili used the platform to explain the concept, principle, methods, and processes behind the introduction of the Public Procurement Reform programme. She also provided insights into the monetization policy of that administration, the work of the economic management team of the Obasanjo administration in which she was a key member, among other issues. She equally spoke of the intended benefits of the programme to the economy and society, the risks involved and opportunities inherent in the implementation as well as ways to minimize and maximize the opportunities.

Oby was an interviewer's delight. It was Oby Ezekwesili's first major radio interview in her job on public procurement reforms in Nigeria as Senior Special Assistant to President Obasanjo. The programme made two editions of Eagle Square and was broadcast several times on the network service of Radio Nigeria. Besides, key issues raised by Oby in the interview in each of the editions made headlines in our major national news and programmes.

I remember that after the interview on that wonderful day, as I was walking her to the car, Oby began to ask me some personal questions about my background, like what I studied in the University, how long I had been on the job, etc., adding that I impressed her with my knowledge of the issues and the good questions I asked that brought out her explanations clearly. I responded the best way I could.

My story underlines the need to prepare adequately for an interview and source for quality guests who have done or are doing something. Interviewing a knowledgeable person requires more than enough preparation. As a result of that encounter, she later invited me over to her office and offered me a better job. I was appointed to head the media and public affairs section in the Budget Monitoring and Price Intelligence Unit in the State House, Presidential Villa, under her leadership in May 2004.

My work essentially was to relate with the public, the media and the civil society. By that assignment, I was privileged to have been part of the select group that midwifed the public procurement reform programme of that administration under her leadership. The Budget Monitoring and Price Intelligence Unit later transformed into the Bureau of Public Procurement (BPP) on June 4, 2007 when the Public Procurement Bill was signed into Law by the Yar'adua administration. My work continued with the new BPP in the same capacity until 2008 when I left the country for Harvard University Kennedy School on an executive education programme on public policy and communication.

It should be noted here that working with Oby was tough, pretty tough, but it was a good school for me and a cherished experience. I will share one of such. I resumed at her office and requested for an office with a secretary. I expected a place similar to, if not better than, where I was coming from. Oby starred at me, adjusted her seat, brought out a bag under her seat, opened it, brought out a laptop and handed it over to me. "Now Orji," she said. "This laptop is your seat, your secretary, your messenger and your office, okay? If you want anything about your job, please consult the laptop. Everything you need to function effectively is in here! Any other thing?" she queried. "Madam, but I am not computer literate," I said "Really? That is amazing! A journalist? How have you been functioning? How can you work here? Well, in that case, you are in the wrong place. But since you are already here, you either fall in or you fall out. I am giving you just five days to learn to use that laptop effectively or you go back to where you are coming from okay?" she concluded and focused her attention to a document in front of her. As I left her office with that final verdict, I was in a world of confusion with all kinds of questions and reflections running riot all over my mind. 'Is it not shameful to lose the opportunity to work inside the Presidential Villa on a better job, simply on reasons of incapacity?' I queried myself. It was then that I resolved to fully embrace aggressive adult education on computer literacy. As I took up the challenge, unknown to me, Oby monitored my commitment and efforts as I battled and sweated it out on the Laptop in one corner of the adjoining room to her office, with her Personal Assistant, Adebowale Adedokun, as make-shift instructor. Debo (as I called Adebowale for short) was on my side and at my service. In response to what Oby saw, another five days extension was added. The rest, as they say, is now history.

Back to my earlier story. Before I left to take up the appointment, the reputation of Eagle Square on Radio Nigeria network service was established as a courageous, analytical, insightful and independent public accountability current affairs programme. One reason for this was the quality of guests on each edition of the programme.

For instance, after Ezekwesili, the next was Mallam Nuhu Ribadu. It was his first radio interview after his appointment as Chairman of Economic and Financial

Crimes Commission - EFCC. Others, not in any particular order ,were, Mallam Nasiru El Rufai, first on the demolition of illegal structures in Abuja and secondly for his side of the story over his bribery allegations against Senator Ibrahim Mantu in the National Assembly. Senator Mantu also appeared on the programme to state his own side.

I made efforts to bring the Ikemba of Nnewi, Emeka Odumegwu Ojukwu to give account of his role in the Nigerian civil war, but it was very difficult so I had to go for former Head of State, General Gowon, who instantly responded and appeared on Eagle Square. General Gowon's interview ran into series of editions with very hot and engaging stories of the war. Following the reactions that greeted General Gowon's answers to my questions on his own account of the war, the Ikemba, Emeka Odumegwu Ojukwu invited me to his residence – Independence Layout, Enugu, for his own side of the story on the Nigerian civil war. At that point, editors of major newspapers and magazines were all over me for stories arising from each edition of Eagles Square which made headlines in major national papers.

Apart from the Gowon – Ojukwu accounts of the civil war, I invited Senator Arthur Nzeribe at the peak of the public outcry over the motion he moved on the floor of the Senate, calling for the impeachment of President Obasanjo. I also got the account of Senator Idris Kuta, an influential Senator from Niger State who chaired the controversial Kuta Panel whose report led to the removal of Dr Chuba Okadigbo as President of the Senate. It was on Eagle Square that Senator Kuta (now late) made a statement about the abuse and looting of public treasury, sometimes with impunity, by some public officers in Nigeria.

In answer to my question on transparency and accountability, Senator Kuta said in a very solemn voice: "Orji please listen to me very carefully and mark my words. No public officer goes free, unpunished after embezzling Nigerian money. You cannot steal, loot and eat Nigerian money and go free. The officer may or can escape criminal prosecution, escape police investigations and even resist any form of inquiry. But one thing I have seen that no such officer escape is the punishment." I listened attentively as the eloquent Senator, who was a major power broker in the Senate, continued, " You see, the punishment comes in many forms and dimensions. One of them is ill health. I then asked, "how do you know, Sir?" He replied: " I know because I meet many of them in major hospitals in Germany, London, USA, France, etc. They also tell me about their experiences and that public office is a position of trust, and is not to be abused. I do not know how many politicians know that. Another punishment is through their families." Senator Kuta alleged that public officers who abuse their offices by diverting public funds to serve selfish and family interest only attract calamities upon their families. I was quite numb as Senator Kuta challenged me to look round and show him examples of key public officers who left office and are not in one form of problem or the other except for the few who left public service with honour and integrity. I then asked the reason for the punishment.

His answer was graphic and simple: "Because many of us who abuse public offices forget that we took oath with either Qur'an or the Bible in our hands before assuming the positions. The oath of office is usually administered publicly. We forget as soon as we take up the appointment and then begin to do exactly the opposite of what we pledged. Senator Kuta warned that abuse of public office, which he lamented was common in Nigeria, has very grave repercussions.

He challenged me to carefully take a copy of oath of office and oath of allegiance usually administered to public officers, study it carefully and ponder the meaning. That interaction with Senator Idris Kuta is permanent in my memory, especially when I watch newly appointed public officers take oath of office. I also try to link their performances in office, to the very essence of their oath. I do not know if the Kuta theory is true or false but I took the lesson seriously. Let us closely examine the content of the oath of office:

Oath of Office for public officers

I, ... do solemnly swear/affirm that I will be faithful and bear true allegiance to the Federal Republic of Nigeria; I will discharge my duties to the best of my ability, faithfully and in accordance with the Constitution of the Federal Republic of Nigeria and the law, and always in the interest of the sovereignty, integrity, solidarity, well-being and prosperity of the Federal Republic of Nigeria; that I will strive to preserve the Fundamental

Objectives and Directive Principles of State Policy contained in the Constitution of the Federal Republic of Nigeria; that I will not allow my personal interest to influence my official conduct or my official decisions, that I will to the best of my ability to preserve, protect and defend the Constitution of the Federal Republic of Nigeria; that I will abide by the Code of Conduct contained in the Fifth Schedule to the Constitution of the Federal Republic of Nigeria; that in all circumstances, I will do right to all manner of people, according to law, without fear or favour, affection or ill-will; that I will not directly or indirectly communicate or reveal to any person any matter which shall be brought under my consideration or shall become known to me except as may be required for the due discharge of my duties.

So help me God.

Appearance on Eagles Square became a status symbol for well-known public officers at the centre of controversy or topical issues of public interest. By the time I was leaving the programme, the popularity and reputation of the programme could serve as bank collateral! I do not know what the status of the programme is at the moment, because I hardly have the time to listen as a result of my tight schedule. But the whole point is that the reputation of a programme has a lot to do with its content and the knowledge base of the producer and presenter.

Editorial Writing

The editorial of a media organization represents the independent opinion of the organization on public policies or issues of public interest. The editorial sometimes follows an appraisal of aggregate public opinion and discourse on the subject matter. It also comes as an intervention to set the right agenda capable of promoting the right atmosphere for constructive discussions, conversations, mobilization of public opinions and discourse in favour or against a particular issue of public interest within the realms of logic, reason, justice, fairness, equity and good conscience.

For the broadcast media, especially Radio Nigeria, the editorials come in the form of news commentary or news analysis. Until 1999, it was called News Analysis. It represents both our opinion as a public broadcaster funded by the Nigerian taxpayer as well as the independent views expressed courageously on daily basis in the broadcast media as a core social responsibility in advancement of human liberty, knowledge development and public good. There are listeners on radio who wait for nothing else during the daily major news broadcast except to listen to the News Commentary or News Analysis which normally follow the news.

Editorials or commentaries help to put both the government and the governed in check in the exercise of their authority, powers, influence and responsibilities. The reputation of a media organization, either print or electronic, is defined by the quality of its editorials and commentaries. This explains why media organizations in

Nigeria like the Guardian, This Day and Punch Newspapers rank, by my estimation, quite high in that order in the quality, boldness and independence of their editorials on national issues. As I write this page, The Guardian Editorial of Wednesday January 22nd, 2014 on Same Sex Prohibition Law (Anti Gay) is a prime example.

For the broadcast media, developing and writing news commentary or analysis can be interesting but it requires discipline. Looking back, I think I was a good student of Uche Uwechue, one of the best I ever worked with as Controller, Current Affairs at the Broadcasting House, Ikoyi in the early 1990s. Uche Uwechue will teach his students, drawn largely from the Network News Room, that writing a good news commentary or news analysis required the following steps:

- Good knowledge of the subject matter enhanced by reading, research and exposure to all sides of the issue.
- Begin with a catchy and inviting introduction.
- Give a brief background and history of the problem or subject matter.
- Explain the consequences to public good, order or public interest.
- Recall previous efforts to deal with the issue and why it failed.
- Provide an overview and motive of the current effort.
- Explain why the new policy is good or not.

- Highlight the risks (if any) on the way of implementation.
- Assign duties or burden to those behind the new policy.
- Provide advice or guidance.
- Conclude.

With these basic steps, I was able to try my hands on writing commentaries and over time became a regular contributor to news commentaries on the Network Service. It was an additional responsibility that required a lot of time, efforts, knowledge, discipline and interest. News commentary is one area that separates the men from the boys among news and programmes staff.

It was and still is an exercise to which many are called but few are chosen. It attracts zero remuneration and only a few care to make the effort. But I was just satisfied with the fact that I wrote the commentary for the day. However, the experience came handy one day in 1996 when I was invited to appear for an interview for promotion. I was among eleven officers shortlisted to compete for just two positions. Out of the eleven of us, by every consideration, one person was sure to get that position, leaving just one position for the ten of us.

I was the most junior of the ten in an era when seniority in service was a major advantage in public sector promotions. And I needed that promotion because no one was sure how long it would take for another opportunity to come knocking. Besides, I learnt quite early in life that a patient dog in Nigeria eats no bone any longer because the first set of dogs will eat the meat and the bone. I was therefore not prepared to gamble with the only opportunity I was sure of.

Therefore, in preparing for the interview, I decided to go with not just my credentials but with two big files containing copies of news commentaries written by me and which had been broadcast. Since the files were bulky, I packed them into one carton and sealed it. On the day of the interview, when I came into the venue with a carton, everyone became curious to know what was inside. I refused to disclose it and diverted their attention by saying that I was going on a journey after the interview.

I refused to disclose the content of the carton because that information was meant for the panel inside and not for my competitors. When I was called, I moved in with the carton. A member of the panel asked me: "Orji, why are you bringing a carton?" I replied, "Sir, ten well qualified officers are here to compete for just one position. The way I see it Sir, I think the situation on ground demands more than just presentation of certificates to the panel. The content of the carton will be required in the course of the interview Sir." All the members of the panel starred at each other and burst into a prolonged laughter. I stood by and watched with a straight face. When their laughter subsided, the chairman asked me to take a seat, open the carton and explain. I took a seat, opened the carton and took my time to untie each of the files containing bundles of copies of news commentaries while all the members watched me with rapt attention and subdued silence.

When I was done, I began my explanation, "Mr Chairman, members of the panel, in addition to my schedules and duties, these news commentaries were written by me at my spare time. Each of these scripts was broadcast on the network service on the date on each of the scripts over these years and period under review. I did all these as additional responsibilities in support of our news operations." The panel looked at each other, asked me to stand, take a bow and leave.

I do not know what happened and how, but I was among those promoted. In broadcasting, one needs to move outside one's comfort zone sometimes, think outside the box all the time and take additional interests and responsibilities to confront and overcome challenges.

My interest in writing news commentaries and analysis outside the normal call of duty had other benefits. It brought me quite closer to and created some form of intimacy with, the top management staff of the Federal Radio Corporation of Nigeria. Many of these officers, were people that one would not be ordinarily expected to meet with. But when a news commentary is on air, especially if it is on key national issues of contemporary public interest, you never can imagine who is listening and for what reason.

Many of the officers, retired and serving, take pains to call to express constructive opinions on the commentary or analysis. In spite of the way the opinions go, they end up commending me and parting with words of encouragement and advice. The Zonal Director, Radio Nigeria, Lagos, Ikenna Ndaguba, was in that category. I got closer to him through this aspect of the work. On his death at the age of 76, I wrote the commentary, which was more of a tribute broadcast on the network service of Radio Nigeria on the day of his burial. The commentary cum tribute is reproduced below:

LIFE AND TIMES OF IKENNA NDAGUBA

By

Orji Ogbonnaya Orji

All roads lead to the commercial city of Onitsha, Anambra State today as Nigerians from far and near travel to the ancient town to bid farewell to one of the greatest broadcasters in the nation's history, Ikenna Ndaguba, who died recently in Abuja at the age of 76. The burial today is the climax of series of events put in place by the national burial committee to create opportunities for Nigerians to pay respect, to Chief Ndaguba and condole with his family.

Ikenna Ndaguba's long meritorious career in broadcasting began at the dawn of Nigeria's independence when he joined the then Eastern Nigerian Broadcasting Service, Enugu in 1960. He was the first trained voice to establish the regional station in the minds of the people on air as a presenter. His voice commanded so much

146

authority in the ENBS news and programmes that, within a short time, Ikenna Ndaguba became a household name throughout the Eastern Region.

It was therefore not surprising when he was selected as one of the best voices in the country to commence the External Service of the Nigerian Broadcasting Corporation in 1963 when the country required aggressive media campaign to sell her post-foreign policy to the outside world. For his exploits in the media industry for over four decades, the name Ikenna Ndaguba could easily be compared with such name like Rotimi Williams in the legal profession.

For instance, while in service from 1960 to 1995, he held several high ranking positions from the era of Nigerian Broadcasting Service through the period of Nigerian Broadcasting Corporation until the time when the national radio became the Federal Radio Corporation of Nigeria. The climax was when he rose to be the Managing Director, FRCN Lagos in the early 90s.

During this period, he pioneered the introduction of FM broadcasting in Nigeria and emerged as the first General Manager of the first FM Radio station in Nigeria, Radio Nigeria 2, at 45, Martins Street, Lagos. While in service, he received several trainings in reputable radio and television stations around the world, including the BBC and the VOA, served in the boards of several media organizations and belonged to many professional associations including the Broadcasting Organizations of Nigeria.

It was Ikenna Ndaguba's generation of broadcasters that developed and institutionalized the basic ethics, codes of conduct and rules of engagement for the broadcasting profession in the country. During their time, mistakes such as factual or grammatical errors either in the news or programmes while on air was regarded as taboo and attracted severe punishment. In fact, their era believed that broadcasting was a noble profession built on discipline, competence, creativity, innovation and knowledge.

His generation built the public confidence that whatever is heard on radio is the only truth free from error or prejudices.

In appreciation of his valuable contributions to the profession and national development, he was conferred with a national honour of Member of the Federal Republic, MFR. But if Ikenna Ndaguba made impact while in service, such impact was better appreciated when he retired from active service. He became a known face and known voice in virtually all Presidential functions as Master of Ceremony to the extent that his presence was one condition that defined the dignity of many state functions.

But the difference between Ikenna Ndaguba and other national celebrities was his exceptional passion to make contributions to the development of his native community. In appreciation, he was inducted into the prestigious Agbalanze Society of Onitsha and conferred with the famous Ozo Title of "Onwa". This probably *explains why the Onitsha Traditional Council has strictly indicated that Ikenna Ndaguba's burial today will witness a traditional and cultural celebration of an illustrious son.*

As his casket is lowered today, the broadcast industry and the entertainment world in Nigeria have lost a great talent, renowned broadcaster, orator, writer and mentor. However, the challenge before the industry is how to ensure that the virtues and legacies which people like Ikenna Ndaguba left behind, such as using the media to uplift the people and unite the nation, are nurtured and sustained.

The commentary attempted to highlight those qualities and training which early broadcasters strove to bequeath to the profession. These included excellence in operations, zero tolerance for error, discipline, mentoring and passion for community service. Ikenna Ndaguba's generation of broadcasters represented these and more. During their era, standards were high.

Chapter 10

Broadcasting and Development

In 1995, the Abacha Administration set up the Vision 2010 Presidential Committee with a specific mandate to define Nigeria's development strategy between that time and the year 2010. I was nominated to serve in that Committee as one of the representatives of the Media Industry in Nigeria. I think I made the list because I won the Nigeria Media Merit Award that year.

Others who served on that committee on the platform of the media included Frank Aigbogun, former Editor-in-Chief of Vanguard Newspapers, the Chairman and Publisher of ThisDay Newspapers, NdukaObaigbena, Honourable Abike Dabiri, then of the NTA, now in the National Assembly as well as my colleague, Bisi Olatilo, then of the FRCN and now Chief Executive Officer of Biscom Communications. I served in the Media sub-committee, as well as the sub-committee on Population, chaired by the then Director General of Nigerian Institute for Social and Economic Research, Professor Dotun Phillips. It was my first major exposure to inside issues around Nigeria's development plans, policies and programmes.

During the deliberations, I did make the point that media practitioners understand development issues differently. I argued that for public officers, development is all about policy formulation and implementation. For instance, those of them who are economists are concerned about gross domestic products, national wages and incomes, resource allocation, inflation, interest rates, jobs, monetary policies, debt and budget management issues. They equally worry about how these and more micro- and macro-economic issues interface with the economy. They pay little or no attention to how these policies translate to food on the table of average Nigerian families. For public officers from the political class, especially in Nigeria, development is more about power, influence, legislations, and authoritative distribution of resources to serve political motives. To them, development is a struggle on who gets what and how. The political class shows little or no interest to development needs and priorities.

But the media views development in terms of visible impact and value added to the lives of people. The media equally defines development with the realms of the greatest good for the greatest number. The media campaign over the implementation of the independent power project, the reconstruction of major Federal highways and the state of public hospitals are few examples.

In the search for impact, the media is interested in interrogating the effectiveness of the policy implementation. Media reports would therefore raise important questions about how policies, programmes and legislations connect directly with the people; questions like the following: What is the effectiveness or otherwise of the design and implementation strategy? Is the policy working, if not, why? What about prudence in the utilisation of resources designed to implement the policy? In the search for impact, the media will continue to raise questions and demand explanations. It will continue to exercise its fundamental role of monitoring the society at all stages of implementation.

My point then and even now remains that in policy formulation and implementation in Nigeria, the role of the media is often ignored. It is important to note that the media is more inclined to work with a national development strategy built on a work-plan with activities that are specific, measurable, achievable, and relevant and time-bound. Under this circumstance, the outcomes, key performance indicators and outputs can be easily identified and monitored. It would then be easier for the media, especially radio and television because they are nearer, more convenient, and have wider reach, to carry out the following functions which are critical to national development.

The media has the function of identifying and exposing citizens to development challenges facing them in their immediate localities. Examples are, the need for hospitals, health centers, schools, roads, water, security, markets, etc. For instance, it was the local radio that first broke the story of the collapsed Itigidi Bridge that connects Ebonyi and Cross River State and the poor condition of Lagos-Ore-Benin Road. The outbreak of cholera in Zamfara, Kano and other parts of the North, resulting in loss of many lives, was made known by the media about June-July 2013. The media interest drew the attention of government and international community, including the World Health Organisation. The media also broke the story of snake bites in some communities in Gombe State.

Another duty of the media is to simplify development issues for the people in the languages they understand and speak fluently. The media develops specific programmes in local languages such as Ibo, Yoruba, Hausa, Tiv, Efik, Ijaw, Fufude, etc. In the early 1980s, Radio Nigeria, Enugu created an early morning music chit-chat programme in Ibo called *Ngwon-ngwo* (mixed delicacy). The programme, presented with humour by a natural comedian, Jevas Chukwuemezie (now late), was such a popular programme that it became a major channel of reaching the people at the grassroot. A similar programme in the early 1980s, known as 'Tombo Connection' by the then Anambra Broadcasting Corporation (ABC 1) was another great programme that attracted a very large audience. Today, such programmes like Political Platform, produced and broadcast by the Ray Power FM, and *Hembelembe*, another grassroot audience participation programme by the Love FM in Abuja are great programmes with a large audience. These programmes identify specific development challenges and put the challenges directly in the public domain for advocacy and attention.

The broadcast media identifies the community representatives directly responsible for fixing the identified development challenges. The radio or television mentions names of elected or appointed local, state or federal representatives whose attention should be drawn to the issues. These include ministers, members of the National Assembly and others and they are usually invited to offer explanations and insights on the issues.

The broadcast media develops programmes that build the confidence of the ordinary citizen at the grassroot to demand for good governance as a matter of right and responsibility. The radio and television use grassroot programmes and news to educate the people on the true relationship between public officers and the citizens that they should be seen as servants of the people, not masters.

The media provides a familiar platform for the ordinary citizen and their representatives to share information on development priorities relevant to the people. This is through creation of talk or chit-chat programmes.

The media serves as a vehicle for social mobilization, education and enlightenment on development policies and programmes. For instance, such development issues as HIV/AIDs campaign, immunization, voter education, birth control, girl-child education, etc., are better promoted using radio and television. An example is the Aso Radio call centre service deliberately set up for civic education on development programmes.

The media is responsible for the promotion of self-help approach to development. The concept of self-help developed when it became clear to most communities in Nigeria and indeed the West African sub-region that the era when government was jack of all trade and master of all was gone. Self-help development therefore became a response to the inability of government to fund all development projects as a result of competing demands on the dwindling resources.

It then became clear to some communities that except and until they help themselves, help may not come soon. Under the self-help development concept, many communities, through town union associations, individuals and group philanthropy, began to explore the options of pulling their resources together to provide roads, water, electricity, and other social amenities.

The self-help development concept turned around some communities like Abiriba in South Eastern Nigeria into what many refer to as "small London". A visit to Abiriba will confirm that in terms of infrastructure, the community is a model of self-help development efforts.

Many communities around the area have also adopted the idea. Today, self-help development approach has become a viable alternative. And radio and television have no doubt been the most efficient medium to the advancement of this emerging development approach. To do this effectively, the need to develop rural-based news and programmes content becomes fundamental. The agitation for Community Radio equally becomes important.

The broadcast media serves as agent of conflict prevention, management and resolution. Radio and television, more than any other media are better positioned to serve as agents of conflict prevention, management and resolution. This is one area in which the editorial policies of government-owned radio and television stations in Nigeria are misunderstood. For example, in times of national crisis such as civil disturbances, communal conflicts, riots, protests, and other forms of social unrests, the government-owned media has the responsibility of exercising professional moderation in reporting the issues. This professional moderation is demonstrated with every effort to reduce tension in the land and bring such conflicts to an early end. During such situations, efforts are made to avoid sensationalism and gender, religious and ethnic colouration or primordial sentiments in the presentation of the news reports emanating from the crisis.

I recall that around 1992, there was a major civil disturbance in Kaduna State. Many lives and valuable properties were lost in the crisis which lasted for about a week. At the peak of the conflict, many stories filtered into the network newsroom. The stories were all about killings and destruction of properties. One of the reports contained details of how many Muslims and Christians that were killed, how many Igbos and Hausas lost their lives and how areas of the city either dominated by Christians or Muslims were affected.

When the report was sent to the editor for approval, he immediately called me to rewrite the story without missing out the facts. But the editor warned that all forms of ethnic, religious and primordial identification in the story must be dropped. I wanted to know why. "My friend, listen," he began, "if you say that 10 Christians and 7 Muslims were killed, the tendency is for the Christians to seek revenge to either balance the equation or cause more havoc and vice versa. On the other hand, if you say 10 Igbos and 7 Hausas were killed, you will be escalating the crisis as the side that lost more people will head for a reprisal attack. You must also be silent on which area of the city suffered more damage in order to protect the other peaceful areas from attack. Please focus your story on the efforts of security agencies to return calm and normalcy to the city." The editor commanded. I obeyed the instruction. I then rewrote the story to read as follows:

"A dusk to dawn curfew has been imposed in Kaduna, following civil disturbances that broke out in the city yesterday. A Radio Nigeria Correspondent in Kaduna reports that 17 people died in the incident while property valued at millions of naira were damaged. Our correspondent also reports that combined efforts of the Armed Forces, the Police and other security agents who have been working to restore normalcy to the ancient city is yielding desired result."

When I re-submitted the story, the editor then sat me down to a conversation between teacher and student. "Orji, we in radio cannot afford to go the way of newspapers." "You see," he continued, "the newspapers are looking for sensational headlines to sell their papers and make money.

The more the tension in their stories, the more attention it generates, the more patronage they get. But radio, especially government-owned radio, has the responsibility to protect, preserve and promote the society for development. Remember, development cannot happen in the atmosphere of conflict. For the FRCN (Radio Nigeria), the mission is to *Uplift the People and Unite the Nation*. This responsibility is more in times of national crisis." The editor ended his sermon and requested me to return to my seat. That encounter exposed me more to the role of the media in sustenance of national security and development. The encounter was equally expository as to the basic reasons why government-owned radio and television stations target their editorial policies towards achieving peace, national unity, and cohesion for national development.

Nigeria is currently battling with complex problems of insecurity arising from the Boko Haram insurgents in parts of the North as well as kidnappings and armed robbery in parts of the South. This is in addition to series of communal conflicts, thuggery and cultism, to mention but a few. What is not very clear to many is the existence of comprehensive communication strategy by respective media organisations in reporting the security issues.

From the media reports so far, we appear to attribute the issues of development such as access to education, health, food, housing, jobs, and basic social amenities to the root causes of the insurgency. Development experts would agree that the argument appear valid. However, the media, especially radio and television, has an important role to play at this time. A comprehensive media strategy has become an urgent professional option. The strategy has to pay attention on building the confidence of the public on efforts by the state to guarantee security of lives and property. Secondly, the strategy must have content on mobilizing public opinion, solidarity and consensus in support of security agencies whose call of duty require that they remain awake when we are all fast asleep. A media-led public solidarity can cheer them to victory. Lastly, the time for the media to help build strong alliance among the political class and other categories of elites against terrorism is now. The role of the media is key in the war against terrorism as we saw in US invasion of Iraq after the 9/11. The western media, led by the US press, mobilized the minds, attention and solidarity of all Americans and their allies in support of officers and men, leading the military aggression in Iraq. The war on terror can be won if we can 'use the pen to reduce the pain'.

It has therefore become necessary for the media to evolve a suitable communication strategy derived from existing editorial policies and house styles so as to guide media reporting of the security issues.

The approach at the moment appears to create more problems than it is intended to solve. We must avoid escalating the problem through sensationalism, ethnic, religious and primordial colouration of the issues. In this direction, the tendency to use photographs to deepen the contents of reports needs to be professionally re-examined. While the use of visuals and photographs are quite necessary, it is worrisome that some media organisations, in their efforts to develop fresh angles to the stories from the killings, appear to ignore the sensitivity and pain such reports could cause their target audience. Besides, we need the existence of the society to practice the profession. I am suggesting responsibility, not censorship.

The media, especially the electronic media, must play active roles in governance and institutional reforms. In a country like Nigeria, which is emerging from years of military dictatorship, the role of the media to draw national and international attention to the reform of political and governance institutions are key to national development. This is an advocacy the media needs to champion in association with the civil society. The advocacy has to be based on suitable content, targeted at state actors and non-actors. The reform must begin with attitudinal change that tends to underline the importance of sanctions and incentives. A society where bad conduct is rewarded openly cannot make much progress as there will be no incentives for people to behave well in accordance to existing laws, rules, and procedure. The introduction of several reform programmes by government should be well-covered by the media so as to help the public to understand the issues, principles, focus, roles and benefits.

The media also needs to embrace all opportunities for capacity building with regards to development issues. The common attitude of viewing such opportunities as irrelevant or of less priority needs to be discouraged. The knowledge gap in the media on contemporary development issues is simply too wide. It is only regular exposure to trainings that can help narrow the gaps.

The media has the responsibility of setting an agenda for social change. One way of achieving this is through informed research, familiarity with development priorities based on need assessment, information and analysis. In-depth research on the issues would help the media set an agenda based on knowledge. It saves both the government and the people from a syndrome in the development sector referred to as "planning without facts".

Chapter 11

The New Media and Rules of Engagement

The emergence of new media in Nigeria and most African States did not just happen. It was facilitated. The new media regime has an interesting history in media evolution and transition in this part of the world. In the 1990s, the internet culture was unknown to the broadcasting industry in Nigeria and many other African countries. Even mobile phones were non-existent, at least to the knowledge and use of an average Nigerian. If cell phones existed at all, it was in the hands of the very few as an exclusive preserve.

At that time, most African nations were battling with liberation from one form of oppressive regime or the other. In Nigeria, the struggle was for liberation from military dictatorship and return to civil rule, while in countries like

South Africa, the end of Apartheid was all that mattered. During this period too, the broadcasting industry was a government monopoly in Nigeria. I am not aware of the existence of any private radio or television station up till 1998. It was a period under the military administration, where most Nigerians depended only on government-owned radio and television stations for information on people and events. Broadcast media operations on daily basis were on analogue.

Freedom and access to information were restricted by various military decrees with severe sanctions for any violations. The opportunity for Nigerians to access information in order to make decisions and informed choices was hardly available. As *Media in Africa*, a publication on the state of the media in the continent in the 1990s, aptly captured it, "chances for ethical journalism was a dream, an illusion." Most Africans were not just blighted by underdevelopment but also severely malnourished in terms of availability and quality of information. It was an era when media development in most African countries was almost everywhere subjected to whims and caprices of oppressive regimes, self-interested elites who had captured power for personal gain, using combinations of force and nationalism to do so."

The researched publication represented a status report of the media in Africa and an outcome of an international conference on media development in Africa held in Windhoek, Capital of Namibia. It attempted to provide justification for the bondage that frustrated media development in most African States at that time. "Many post-colonial African States, including Nigeria, had freed themselves from foreign rule in 1960s only to evolve into systems where authoritarian regimes controlled every key institution of power such as the parliament (where any existed), public service, security services, electoral systems and the judiciary. In the case of the media industry, the oppressive regimes did not just control but seized it." The total control and seizure involved coercion or co-option, repressive laws and political domination.

However, following the failure of these oppressive regimes (common in most African countries at the time) to deliver on viable development projects capable of responding adequately to the increasing hunger, disease, deprivation and hopelessness that faced the citizens, the regimes were confronted with increasing pressure, and popular demands for liberation by their respective citizens. The popular agitations were on the increase at a time the international community was beginning to withdraw support for dictatorial regimes.

The fall of oppressive regimes in Eastern Europe which set the stage for the eventual collapse of the Berlin Wall boosted the struggles in most African countries, including Nigeria. *The Media in Africa* publication noted that, "The citizens' agitation for change in the 1990s was ripe to happen, even in apartheid South Africa, the form and the timing of change were uneven around the continent with popular citizen's demand for elections and their consequences differing between countries."

The 1990s witnessed gradual but steady wind of change from the impunity of the centralized authoritarianism, giving way to strong waves of democracy with far-reaching and positive implications for the development of journalism in most countries on the continent. It was also an era that witnessed deeper involvement of development partners such as the UNESCO, the World Bank and the UNDP in extending support to building the capacity of media professionals, and the deliberate exposure of media professionals to global developments in the industry.

These interventions led to the first important conference convened by UNESCO on the role of a free, independent and pluralists Press in sustaining democratization process in Africa, held in Windhoek, Namibia. At the conference, journalists and broadcasters in Africa took a common stand that clearly defined and pursued free, independent and plural press built on high ethical standards consistent with global best practices. The report of the conference was called Windhoek Declaration. The report of that conference fed into other similar reports that helped to form the comprehensive Press Freedom Document endorsed in 1993 by the United Nations General Assembly. The development led to the UN declaration of May 3 every year as World Press Freedom Day. That UN declaration was adopted by all member countries including Nigeria. This global positive development in the practice of journalism provoked internal positive reforms in our country that pushed down many dangerous barriers erected in the way of free media practice and development in Nigeria by oppressive regimes.

In spite of these reforms, I remember that even as at 1998, the internet culture, information and communications technology were still not commonly in use in government-owned media organizations, including Radio Nigeria. All our news and programmes were in analogue. Reporters had to send or submit stories handwritten or dictate same through telephone for the reporter in the newsroom to write down and type with typewriters – the types we normally say were probably left behind by Lord Lugard when he was leaving Nigeria after independence.

I recall quite clearly my first visit to the United States on September 23rd, 1998. I was part of the media entourage of the then Head of State, General Abdulsalami Abubakar's visit to the United States. The General was on his way to attend the UN General Assembly. It was an important visit for Nigeria, given international concerns on the future of Nigeria, following the death of Abacha and General Abubakar's pledge to heal the injuries inflicted on the country by the annulment of June 12, 1993 elections which the Abacha regime failed to address, and more importantly, the pledge of an early return to civil rule. The visit was to provide information on these issues to the international community, using the UN platform. But as a matter of courtesy, General Abubakar had to stop over in Washington to see and brief the President of the United States at the time, Bill Clinton.

The Nigerian Embassy in Washington had booked the entourage into a five-star hotel in the heart of Washington

DC. My first major contact with the internet and an ICT environment was on that visit. After we were checked into the rooms, I decided to use the rest room before joining my colleagues for a group lunch downstairs. Immediately I entered the rest room, the door locked and all the lights went off instantly. I grabbed the telephone hung on one side of the rest room, but it was dead as well. I stood there confused, began to knock frantically on the door but no one was nearby to help. I had to perch on one corner of the bath tub while listening attentively to hear if anyone was passing by.

A housekeeping staff knocked at the door an hour later and I quickly answered but she apologized and went away thinking I said I didn't want to be disturbed. No one came again until two hours later, when my colleagues who did not see me at the group lunch came to search for me. "Where has Orji gone to in a country he has never visited before? Are you sure that '*Okoro* boy' has not escaped?" These were the likely questions in the minds of the rest of the team as they all resolved to come searching for me. '*Okoro*' is a common name people from other tribes call an Ibo person to make fun of the 'Ibo claim' of being wiser and smarter than other tribes. In that delegation, I think Chris Ngwu, the NTA State House Correspondent and I, were the only Ibos in the midst of others from other parts of Nigeria. At that time, it was a common occurrence for some young Nigerians who had any slightest opportunity to travel out to developed countries like the United States to run away, citing the military rule in Nigeria as an excuse.

These and more concerns came up during the group lunch.

They had no idea that I was a victim of clash of civilizations, victim of a fight between analogue and digital technology, victim of a war between ancient and modern. However, I was told that many of my colleagues argued that, "Orji is a totally undiluted Nigerian! Orji can never wish to live abroad especially where no pounded yam and egusi soup were easily available." They resolved to come on a search to find out what had happened.

As soon as they knocked on the door, I screamed loud in 'Nigerian Pidgin English' to avoid the mix up that made the other person run way. *"Old boy, make una come! Oyibo door don jam person inside oh! Make una open the door! The door don jam oh!"* I shouted several times on top of my voice. They contacted the reception and help came. The hotel staff profusely apologized and asked if I was told that the hotel was fully computer automated. I said I wasn't told, that perhaps the waiter thought I was used to it.

My other colleagues said that the waiter that checked them in took enough time to explain to them how to use the facilities in the room. My colleagues were lucky that the waiters, knowing that they came from Africa, where the ICT culture was either very low or non-existent, took them through the procedures. From the guide, it became clear that all the facilities in the room; the doors, the lights, the television, the telephones, refrigerators and music player were connected to a computer device beside the bed. I learnt to use the computer device but with extra care and caution, given the horrifying experience I had passed through.

But the knowledge was not enough to carry this timid 'analogue journalist' from Africa through all the facilities in the fully automated hotel at the center of Washington DC. At night, I hardly sleep with lights on. And so I tried to apply my newly acquired American computer technology to switch off the lights as I retired to bed. But no way! All but one stubborn light which was directly on top of the bed went off in spite of all efforts. I then remembered Chinua Achebe's African proverb in *Things Fall Apart*: "If a bird learns to fly without perching, the hunter has no option than to learn to shoot without aiming." I immediately applied Nigerian commonsense, climbed on the table, used one of the towels in the room, tied the light and shut it out completely. As a result, darkness enveloped the room and I slept off.

My story reflects the experiences of most journalists in developing countries including Nigeria in the 'Stone Age' era of media practice before the emergence of internet and information and communication technology which now drive the New Media revolution and explosion in the profession.

The New Media Influence

Information and Communications Technology have positively revolutionalised the communications industry, including broadcasting, in many ways. With ICT, there is now a convergence between computing, communications, content and mobility to offer users better access, higher productivity, ownership, time management and user-convenience. The emergence of ICT culture in the media industry has expanded opportunities for capacity development, wealth creation, reshaped the media world and redefined possibilities.

The ICT development in the media industry, especially broadcasting, has widened opportunities for knowledge sharing and learning, as well as the confidence to face to the dynamics of the industry and challenges of change. In developing countries like Nigeria, where transparency, accountability and good governance remain a challenge, the new media platforms driven by ICT have become easier avenues to communicate, find out what we need, why we need them, when, if others need them too and join forces to agitate for those needs to be provided, compare lessons learnt, all at our own convenience and sometimes, within seconds. The new media has built newsrooms in our palms and broadcasting houses in our homes and living rooms. It has reduced the chances of dependency on other sources and broken barriers between professions. Engineers now see the need to cooperate with historians to ascertain how each other's experiences can be of benefit in crossing barriers and overcoming obstacles. Most importantly, the new media has completely changed the way we communicate with each other and has reduced the world into one global village.

Although computer ownership and internet access are still not common in Nigeria and most African countries, this is mitigated by mobile internet access which is on the rise. With mobile cell phones, and access to new media platforms, a flurry of ideas becomes handy, affordable and convenient, thereby bridging information gaps. With mobile phones and internet access, the journalist, as well as other citizens, are in a world of information, making it easy for them to report, inform, educate and entertain one another on a wide range of issues. Popular among new media platforms are Facebook, Twitter, YouTube, blogs and on-line social media platforms such as Saharareporter.com, PremiumTimes.com etc.

At a time, government-owned broadcast media organizations appeared unprepared to rise to the challenges posed by deregulation of the industry, but the ordinary citizens of countries in Africa have developed more than enough confidence in the new media, depending more on the social media for information on issues around them. This has given rise to what is now commonly known as "Citizen Journalism".

At a training on Strategic Media Relations and Management I attended recently at the Lagos Business School, Victoria Island, Lola Odedina, the Group Corporate Communications Manager of Guaranty Trust Bank told the class, made up of very Senior Information and Public Relations Managers, that the number of Nigerians who depend on the new media for access to information and other uses may have risen above seventy-five million, representing half of Nigerian's population. She doubted if any traditional media organization has that number of audience at the moment. From her statistics, over 40 million Nigerians depended on the internet for information while mobile broad band subscriptions as at 2012 stood at over fifteen million. She predicted that the new media will soon become the major means of communication, given the growing interest in its usage ad application by both public and private sectors.

Lola however warned that embracing the new media without a strategy like we have done in Nigeria is like a man jumping naked into the river with neither basic knowledge of how to swim nor float. She recommended the following rules of engagement of Social Media:

- Provide honest, verifiable and dependable information.

- Interaction must be short, civil, polite and courteous.

- Ensure frequent and regular updates.

- Sustain attention by expanding interaction to other areas.

- Do not abuse or retaliate when abused.

- Keep the interaction on track through constructive responses all the time.

- Decline comments politely on issues you neither have information nor competence.

- Appreciate your followers each time even when provoked.

173

My first global contact and exposure on how far information and communications technology have shaped information and human relations was at the 17th World Congress on Information Technology held in Amsterdam, Netherlands from May 25th to May 27th 2006 . I attended the event as Special Adviser to the Minister of Information and Communication. At the World Congress attended by over 2000 captains of commerce and industry, government leaders, academics, the media and civil society drawn from about 80 countries, we were exposed to global impacts of ICT, the new innovations, policies and how this has advanced humanity to another new level.

I took time to visit all the pavilions such as eGovernment, eBroadcasting, Energy, Water, Creative Industries, Mobility, Health, Cyber Security, and Inclusion. Each of these pavilions made a show of the latest innovations and inventions from various countries. Leading nations in ICT like Japan, United States, UK, Germany, Korea, Malaysia, Singapore, India and Saudi Arabia were there. The Nigerian Communications Commission had its own pavilion too.

I listened to the Head of Partnership Development of the BBC, Bill Thompson, speak to the World Congress on how the broadcasting industry globally was adapting to the new challenges of the digital age. But while I listened to Bill, I wondered if his presentation and global thinking covered the broadcasting industry in my own country because working with the Minister of Information and Communications at the time, I was fully aware of the issues and challenges facing the broadcast media in Nigeria; these problems were certainly different from what Bill Thompson was referring to.

However, in spite of the huge benefits the new media has brought to the broadcasting industry in particular and the media in general, one major problem is the absence of regulation in its conduct and practice. As it stands today, it is difficult for anyone whose rights have been violated in the social media to seek redress. The new media has no room for petitions and recourse mechanisms. This is as a result of the absolute global freedom and clear absence of conflict prevention, management and resolution mechanism.

Another related concern is in the area of quality of standards and code of ethics. Reporting in the new media appear open to all comers, trained and untrained, including those lacking in basic media literacy. This is dangerous, especially in developing and transitional economies like Nigeria.

Chapter 12

The New World Information Order

In 1982, when I joined Broadcasting, the quest for a New World Information and Communications Order was on the global media agenda; a major factor in defining the role of broadcasting in the development of a country like Nigeria. Many in my generation were caught at the middle of the debate with very little knowledge of its origin, objectives and the issues involved.

The debate reflected in all major conferences and workshops as well as in news and programmes bulletins of radio and television stations. As broadcasters, it became important that we were exposed to the issues, the side of the debate that our country finds itself and why, and how the issues would influence our editorial judgements and engagements.

The need for a New World Information and Communication Order began as a debate between the developed, developing and under-developed nations over media representations structures in the operations of the United Nations Educational, Scientific and Cultural Organisation - UNESCO. As one of the most important arms of the United Nations responsible for global development in areas of education with specific intervention programmes in promoting mass literacy, science and culture, most developing and under-developed nations were concerned and were of the opinion that for UNESCO to carry out these functions to the benefit of poor countries, the composition of its media structure and programmes needed to be balanced, fair and equitable for global representation.

The concerns revolved around how UNESCO development programmes would reflect in a comprehensive manner the challenges of development, need and aspirations of poor countries. The developing nations were therefore certain that the global media structure expected to drive UNESCO programmes and projects globally were in no position to appreciate the peculiar problems of poor countries. The debate, which influenced media relations between the rich and poor nations, began within this context around 1970.

An American media scholar, Wilbur Schramm, opened the debate with a survey which revealed that "the flow of news among nations is very thin, much attention is given to developed countries; little or no attention to less-

178

developed countries; important events are ignored, reality distorted and much efforts focused on only negative issues." Another media scholar, Herbert Schiller, supported these findings in a similar research report released in 1970. Schiller's contribution to the debate was on policy. According to him, "developing countries had little or no meaningful inputs into decisions about radio frequency allocations for satellites. Many satellites had military and security applications. And the Agency, Intelsat, set up for international co-operation in satellite communication was also dominated by the United States and other advanced countries with no strong representation from developing countries."

It was against this background, that the Non-Aligned Movement, made up largely of developing countries not aligned with either the United States or the then Soviet Union, resolved to take up the issues as a development agenda for debate within the United Nations. At the meetings of the Non-aligned Movement held in Algiers in 1973; in Tunis in 1976, and later in New Delhi in 1976, the agitation for a New world Information Order among developing nations was key on the agenda of the summits.

The issues in contention included what developing nations considered an unbalanced flow of information from the developed world (especially the United States) to the under-developed countries. Information and entertainment contents of news stories, advertisements, movies and television shows considered to be inappropriate for the third world that originate through the broadcast media in the developed world had indirect but significant effects on mass media.

Other contentious issues included the lopsided politics that guide allocation, distribution and use of radio spectrum where a small number of developed countries controlled almost 90% of the radio spectrum. There were also similar concerns about the allocation of the geostationary orbit (parking spots in space) for satellites. The situation put the developing nations in no position to compete as only a small number of developed countries controlled the available satellites spaces in the orbit; the use of satellites capability by the developed nations were weapons of exploitation of information on crops and natural resources in the Third World at a time when most developing countries lacked the capacity to analyse this data.

Closely aligned to these was the issue of Satellite broadcasting of television signals into Third World countries without prior permission. Many developing countries, including Nigeria, viewed this as a violation of their national sovereignty and threat to peace and security within their territorial boundary.

On the other hand, the position of powerful nations like the United States on the debate for equitable World Information and Communication Order was simply that of resistance. The developed nations considered the agitation as an attempt to create what they felt was avoidable barriers to the free flow of communication required for promotion of global peace and development. The United States, for instance, did not think that the interests of American media corporations with enormous investment interests and potentials for expansion would be adequately protected.

Most of the advanced countries questioned the role of the private sector in communications if the arguments of poor countries are to be sustained. In this context, the New World Information and Communications Order were viewed as dangerous to Press freedom and free flow of information. Developed nations were also concerned that such a global media policy was capable of frustrating international competition, growth and development, especially in the broadcast media where the CNN has already put the world into one newsroom. The developed nations also added that by placing an organization run by governments (as it was the case in most third world countries) at the head, to control global media, it was an open invitation to media censorship.

It concluded that censorship in any form remained antithetical to basic norms of freedom of expression, development and practice of journalism. One of the major casualties of the debate was the withdrawal of the United States from UNESCO on December 31st, 1984 on its perception that UNESCO was behind the global agitation. As at the time of the withdrawal, the United States contribution to UNESCO accounted for about a quarter of the budget of that organisation. The United Kingdom followed suit as a US ally.

But developing nations, especially African leaders, in what seemed to be a reaction to the US and UK action, queued solidly behind UNESCO in the landmark decision called "Yamoussoukro declaration" at the 1985 Summit of the defunct Organization of African Unity, now African Union. In that declaration, the OAU (African Union) identified and resolved that "one of the main keys to solving Africa's development problems lies in recognizing and understanding the importance and strong linkage between effective information management and dissemination in all its forms and national development objectives." Gbemi Bamidele, who had also followed the debate wrote: "Information management and control are not only a positive force for regional and continental integration but also an essential condition for the survival of Africa within the community of nations in the twenty-first (21st) century." And at the centre of information dissemination in poor countries like Nigeria is the broadcast media epitomized by radio and television. In contributing to the debate and its local content for Nigeria, a one time Director General of the Federal Radio Corporation of Nigeria, Eddie Iroh, said it simply, "Information is development and development is information." It was therefore a consistent ethical notion that information remains a shared resource, a social asset and not just a mere commodity.

The increasing importance that the international community attaches to the establishment of a more equitable and just information order is because communication is central to the entire development process; be it economic, social, cultural, educational, scientific or political. According to Mainasara Yakubu Kurfi (2007), "developing countries expect flow of information between the North and the South to be responsive to such considerations as level of development, socio-political environment, national interests, culture and peculiar environments."

But in the present world, a global village driven by knowledge, openness, science and technology, it is unlikely for the media to function within this framework. Information originated by foreign news agencies in developing countries deviates from the ethical norms of the profession with some exceptions, and precepts of developing countries appear like an illusion. This is even more difficult in the midst of growing challenges of poverty, misery, ignorance and disease in most developing countries like Nigeria in spite of abundant natural resources. How then can the global media turn a blind eye to wars and conflicts, electoral and religious crisis, arbitrary abuses of power, human rights violations, environmental degradation and social deprivation common in most developing and so-called poor nations?

It is within this context that the role of the broadcast media in deepening the debate becomes more relevant. It is the responsibility of developing nations to embrace full liberalization and deregulation of the media industry, especially broadcasting. This fundamental step will free the media, especially the broadcasting industry, from government control, economic and editorial censorship as obtainable in developing countries. A free, deregulated

183

independent media in developing countries would be in a position to:

- Tell the African story in a free, original, correct and independent African viewpoint.
- Promote African culture, tradition and values in an African setting.
- Support growth of political and democratic institutions.
- Compete in a global industry driven by content and quality.
- Become innovative, creative and enterprising so as to remain in the business.
- Be in a position to set agenda for development.
- Serve as a reliable agent of change for the society.
- Support conflict prevention, management and resolution mechanism.
- Contribute to global development, peace and security.
- Put Nigeria, Africa and the developing countries in a position to participate in the debate.
- The News Agency of Nigeria and the Voice of Nigeria must be supported to compete globally. The support can come through a deliberate policy intervention as was done in the reforms of the VOA, BBC and Radio Deutsche Welle.

Under the present global media structure, the style, content, approach and presentation of electronic media news flowing in and out of Africa and the developing nations would continue to reflect the interest, preferences, needs and prejudices of the western world. It is therefore not surprising that stories that flow on international media like the CNN, Aljazeera, BBC, VOA, AFP, Reuters and all over the Internet about Nigeria, other African and poor nations largely, reflect crises like HIV/AIDS, terrorism, unemployment, violence, hunger, wars, disaster, etc.

The situation is so bad that except one visits Nigeria or any of the developing nations, the unfortunate international media creation portrays that little or no positive activity goes on in these countries. Even in African countries, governments and citizens view each other with suspicion from the mirror of western media. Most African children born and bred in the western world grow up with this mindset borne out of wrong information and which builds fear and hatred.

In the on-going debate for a new World Information Order, Nigeria shares a common position with member countries in the African Union, being a major victim of international media imperialism until recently. The international broadcast media like CNN, BBC, VOA were first choice destinations for the Nigerian audience for information that they think represent an accurate and balanced account of peoples and events in Nigeria. But with the advent of the new media and private radio and television stations, the audience destination choices have become plural and unrestricted with an open market for choices to shop for any information.

Chapter 13

The Media, Resource Curse and Nigeria's Theory of Development

I was on President Obasanjo's delegation to a United Nations Special Summit on Environment and Development held in Geneva Switzerland around the year 2000. At that time, I was the Radio Nigeria State House Correspondent attached to the President.

On arrival, it became clear to us in the media team, that our travelling allowance could not pay for the same five-star hotel, (Inter-Continental) Geneva, where the President and main delegation were accommodated. The situation clearly separated the men from the boys as we watched helplessly while other high ranking officers checked into the hotel.

We (the media team) therefore decided to take our destiny in our hands. The option available was to look for a hotel in downtown Geneva in an apparent effort to cut our coat according to our size. With the help of embassy officials, we found a cheap hotel for our category. After we checked in and later walked to the bar to have a drink to cool off the stress after a long flight, one white man came towards me and asked, "Where are you guys from?" "Nigeria," I answered. The question was not surprising because everyone around us were white.

So, sighting a group of dark and timid-looking boys was a form of attraction for the whites who looked at us with curiosity. "What are you guys here for; conference or what? my new interrogator continued. "We are here for a conference. I answered." "And when are you guys heading back home?" he again queried.

At this point, Joe Bankole of NAN joined us and became interested in what was going on. "Why are you asking?" I threw back at the guy in a tone that clearly suggested I was getting irritated. "No, don't be annoyed my friend," he pleaded. "No, I m not," I pretended, "but why are you asking," I insisted. "Oh! My friend, I don't want you guys to stay here, okay." There is no money here! Many of you Africans make that mistake. There is a lot of money in Africa, huge money. The owner of this hotel made his cash from Africa in just few months, came back and bought this hotel in cash, okay? Look outside the window," he pointed outside the window showing me buildings, "the choice property there all belong to your brothers from Africa. They come here for weekends with their families, but we see their people suffering from poverty on television, okay. My friend, Africa has resources but the resources is a curse to its citizens. Your leaders are not honest, they are not good. When you finish your conference, please go home, don't stay here, there is no money in Geneva." Then the unsolicited sermon ended. I and my colleagues starred at each other and thanked our preacher for his kind advice as we settled down to some bottles of drinks.

But my colleagues and I began to reflect on the salient issues raised by the man. We also wondered what influenced his preaching. We reflected on his assertions: Africa has resources and their people are poor; we see Africans on television suffering from hunger, diseases and poverty; the hotel we were staying at was bought with money from Africa; African leaders are not good, not honest; go home after your conference, there was no money in Geneva; there is much more money in Africa.

We reasoned that the man was right. These issues dominated our discussions and debate in the bar that evening. From our reflections, our Geneva friend viewed the whole of Africa as one country and our problems common and traceable to resource curse and poor use of resources to improve the citizens' welfare. These issues were in my mind throughout my week-long stay in Geneva. I also attempted to interrogate Nigerians resident in Geneva and other Africans that I met while in that country on these issues.

Many years later, I was part of a robust and intellectual debate on these issues on the 24th of November

2012. The event was the 14th convocation lecture of the
Enugu State University of Science and Technology, South
East Nigeria. Prof. Assisi Asobie was the guest lecturer. The
lecture, which held at the University Auditorium at Agbani
Main Campus, Enugu State, began with a description of
Nigeria as a paradox wrapped in a puzzle; an entity, a
very rich country, wealthy in natural and human resources,
a nation with some of her citizens counted among the
richest persons in the world but with an economy that is
under-developed and the majority of the population
wallowing in abject poverty and misery.

Asobie, a political science Professor, argued that, it is
now conventional wisdom to posit that the possession of
abundance of natural resources does not necessarily
guarantee either fast rate of economic growth or high level
of socio-economic development for a country. On the
contrary, "empirical evidence has been adduced to show
that there is a tendency for resource-rich countries to be
under-developed and for the majority of their citizens to
live below the poverty line as a result of resource curse or
paradox of plenty." The Professor informed his audience
that theories have been propounded to explain the
phenomenal syndrome of resource curse or paradox of
plenty.

The introductory background to the lecture provoked
spontaneous applause from the auditorium filled to
capacity with staff and students of the university. As a media
man with my Geneva prejudices on the issues, I became
more than interested and followed the lecture with all

attention, with specific interest on benchmarking the role of the media. Professor Asobie, who was one time the President of Academic Staff Union of Nigeria Universities (ASUU) drew the audience nearer when he asserted that "the purpose of the lecture was not just to theorize but to reflect and analyze the hitherto beaten paths to Nigeria's national development, examine what have been done, what was being done, what has worked, what has not, what else needs to be done, or done differently and whose duty to do them." My interest in the lecture, driven by my Geneva encounter over ten years before, became deeper when the lecturer attempted to situate the issues on resource curse.

I listened to see how the professor would proffer theoretical explanation to the issues and the role of the media under the circumstance.

THEORY OF RESOURCE CURSE

From the lecture, there are economic and political theories associated with resource curse or paradox of plenty and Nigeria is an interesting case study. The best known is the 'Dutch Disease' hypothesis which explains that when resource-rich countries like Nigeria experience resource boom, the real exchange rate of their national currencies like the Naira, in relation to world currencies, like the US dollar, appreciate. This reduces the global competitiveness of their manufactured and other traded goods. The boom in natural resource therefore leads to contraction of other trading sectors of the economy. He gave the example of Netherlands where increased revenues from natural gas of the North Sea produced negative effects on the Dutch manufacturing sector, resulting in what became known as the "Dutch Disease".

From a development expert, Michael L. Ross, the Dutch Disease model assumes some conditions which do not apply to the economies of developing countries like Nigeria. He posited that the model is predicated on the premise that capital and labour supplies are fixed before a resource boom, concluding that for the economies of developing and under-developed countries like Nigeria, the situation is not exactly the case. It was contended that the economies of developing countries often have a surplus of labour and a manufacturing sector that depends on imports of intermediate goods and rising exchange rates, thereby, making their export goods cheaper, not less competitive. (See Clare Woodside)

Other examples that offer insightful economic explanations to the causes, prevalence and effects of the resource curse or paradox of plenty in a nation like Nigeria include declining or unfair terms of trade; unstable commodity markets; and lack of spillover effects that natural resource extraction like oil and gas, have on other sectors of the economy. As has been noted in the literature, the economic factors do not have inexorable consequences on national economies. The State can mitigate their effects through pre-emptive and proactive policies and action (Woodside)".

From the presentation, one of the different ways of avoiding the economic traps of the resource curse is through

State intervention so as to stop the steady decline in the country's terms of trade with other countries. This can be achieved by investing in the productivity of the natural resource sector and by diversifying the exports. The State can also intervene by providing buffer for their commodities against the vicissitudes of the international commodity markets, by using commodity stabilization funds and appropriate fiscal policies. The State could also use the revenue derived from the commodity price windfall to develop forward and backward linkages in the economy.

To counteract the Dutch Disease, the State could introduce tight fiscal policies; temporarily subsidize the agricultural and manufacturing sectors or place their revenues from the windfall in foreign currencies in order to keep their exchange rates from appreciating (Woodside).

Another interesting part of the lecture was on the Rentier State Model. This was an attempt to provide explanation for why States with much natural resource wealth like Nigeria appear to have similar economic and political development challenges. In particular, oil-rich states are said to have certain common features which constitute obstacles to the consolidation of democracy. (Sandbakken, 2006).

The explanation of the Rentier State theory of development began with the postulation that in periods of boom in commodity prices, countries that are rich in resourses would have a lot of revenue accruing to them; revenue which is not linked to increased productivity by the domestic labour force. Prof. Asobie explained that in such a situation, governments do not necessarily have to tax their citizens to increase government revenue. And since citizens are encouraged to pay little or no tax, the incentive for accountability by government to the citizens becomes very weak because no one will be interested to hold government accountable. In that political context, some governments become myopic and risk-averse; they engage in unproductive rent-seeking and discourage opposition through generous social welfare programmes. In consequence, there is poor economic governance and slow rate of economic growth, leading to continuing under-development (Woodside).

Under the circumstance therefore, a Rentier State may be defined, according to Sandbakken, as a State that depends on rent and demonstrates zero interest for production, a state that receives substantial rents from foreign companies, organizations or governments and do very little in production, capacity development and utilization. A Rentier State is one with an economy that is dominated by rents from abroad and the government is the principal recipient of the rents.

A Rentier State is not necessarily a rent-seeking state, although rent-seeking is usually endemic in a Rentier State where the citizens are more interested on wealth without work. Rent-seeking therefore is the search for financial gain or profit from non-productive economic activities. It is the dependence on state privilege for access to credits, grants, licenses, contracts or monopoly markets. (Sandbakken, 2006:135). And Nigeria is a typical case study.

On the linkage between a Rentier State, development and sustainable democracy, it was argued that there are certain features of Rentier States which make them unlikely to become consolidated democracies. The first feature is that abundant revenues from extractive industries like oil, gas and mining have the tendency to make such a State autonomous from their population. He contended that such States do not have to tax their populations for income. The freedom from taxation reduces to the barest minimum the chances, and basis for citizens to demand accountability from government through their elected representatives.

Another feature Sandbakken added, was that extractive industry revenue accrues directly to the State. "Since the State has discretionary power over how the revenue is spent, it can afford to buy off or repress political opposition. The third feature is that abundant revenue from extractive industries create the kind of social structure that is not favorable to democracy because it creates a society of the very rich and the very poor, resulting in the absence of an independent middle class which can become the bedrock of opposition" (Sandbakken). The existence of a middle class, he argued, in providing a social base for organized opposition is critical because those involved in rent-seeking activities resist democratization. The reason is that it would involve increased transparency and accountability (Sandakken, 2006:138) which is not in their interest.

However, the lecture stated that the Rentier State theory of development has been faulted for its failure to recognize the possibility of economic diversification, which can provide a solution to dependence on the natural resources. Besides, an empirical study of three countries, Algeria, Libya and Nigeria, has shown that though the theory is applicable to African States, it does not apply to them in the same manner, or with equal force.

Overall, the theory provides some useful insight into why and how oil wealth created conditions that were unfavorable to democratization in the three countries. However, the experiences of the three countries show that different parts of the theory apply to the case studies. What the Nigerian case illustrates vividly is how patron-client networks reduce the basis for democratic opposition "as the elites flock around the state in order to enrich themselves" (Sandbakken, 2006:150). This empirical study also shows that the Rentier state theory could be improved by incorporating the agency factor, that is, the role of the state as an agent of development.

Another interesting part of the lecture was Asobie's in-depth analysis of the institutional model of development. He began this part of the lecture by arguing that the institutional model shifts attention from the behaviour of the political elites to the nature of political institutions. The argument is that where there are weak political, bureaucratic and economic institutions, corruption tends to thrive. What then prevails, in spite of resource abundance, is poor economic policy or management. He further posited that since the economy is not protected against commodity price fluctuations, authoritarianism tends to result; and the rate of economic growth declines.

In proffering solutions, Asobie advocated the building of strong institutions; introduction of policies that stimulate economic diversification; institutional mechanism to cushion the effects of price fluctuations; coordinated aggressive taxation; and legitimate steps to institutionalize democracy and its values. Other steps that need to be taken include making deliberate policies to strengthen weak political and economic institutions, and embarking on good political, economic and corporate governance. Asobie also recommended press freedom built on access to information and appropriate responses to combating the resource curse (Woodside).

Nigeria's Theory of Development

The most striking part of the event was an effort by the lecturer to situate the various models within the context of Nigeria's theory of development. It traced Federal Government's efforts at socio-political economic reforms from 1986 through 2003-2007 until 2012 and posited that all the reform efforts in Nigeria reflected an acceptance of a combination of the institutional model, coupled with the rent-seeking theory. "Ibrahim Babangida's administration instituted the structural adjustment programme to address some of the issues raised in these theories. But it was really the administration of Olusegun Obasanjo, during its second term, that instituted a comprehensive reform programme that sought to address the key issues raised in the theory of rent-seeking State and institutional weakness. Obasanjo's reform focused on four main areas: improving the macroeconomic environment, including ensuring fiscal discipline; pursuing structural reforms; strengthening public expenditure management; and implementing institutional and governance reforms, including stepping up the fight against corruption." (Okonjo-Iweala and Osafo-Kwaako, March, 2007)

The lecture however stated that significant challenges that dogged the process led to the failure of the Obasanjo administration's reform programme in translating the benefits of the reforms into welfare improvements for the citizens. Another visible challenge was in the areas of improving the business environment; and extending the reforms to States and Local governments. (Okonjo-Iweala and Osafo-Kwaako)

The lecture went further to concede that currently, the Transformation Agenda of President Jonathan's regime contains proposals similar to the comprehensive economic reform of 2003-2007. The Transformation Agenda embodies the following proposals: pursuing sound macroeconomic policies, including fiscal prudence accompanied by appropriate monetary policy to contain inflation at a single digit; institutionalizing the culture of development planning at all levels of government; and job creation to bring about a drastic reduction in the rate of employment officially put at 21.1 per cent in January 2010. Other measures include prudent public expenditure management designed to reduce the proportion of total budget accounted for by recurrent expenditure; entrenchment of a culture of accountability; instituting a regime of good governance and ensuring the effectiveness of institutions. (Transformation Agenda, Final Report: pp7-9)

These measures are being reintroduced or continued because it is obvious that the issues that the Obasanjo reforms were meant to address still fester; they include poor economic management; rising poverty level; and decline of effectiveness and efficiency of public institutions, resulting in what Asobie called: growth without development.

Before he sat down amidst overwhelming ovations, Prof. Asobie argued that development can only happen in Nigeria if both the government and the governed are prepared to rise to address the resource curse syndrome by using the media to "interrogate" the inexplicit theory of Nigeria's development.

The Role of the Media

Following the lecture to its logical conclusion, my mind went in search of the plethora of roles the media, especially the broadcast media, can play in dealing with key issues identified by the lecturer. How can the media mobilise the citizens, especially the political elites, to build strong consensus among themselves on the appropriate development philosophy and strategy to liberate Nigeria from the resource curse syndrome.

How can the media disentangle itself from what the lecturer described as an ingrained culture of secrecy and confidentiality in public and private affairs which I know are major problems the Nigeria media contend with on daily basis? Has the media done enough in public education, information and enlightenment needed to build business development in order to mobilize adequate domestic capital formation and develop skilled manpower for the economy? Has the media done enough to draw national attention to the consequences of national planning without facts and figures, which is common in Nigeria? What specific programmes has the broadcast media put in place to promote the participation of the people in the electoral process where many hardly vote?

How can the media help to deepen the process of monitoring and evaluation of national priority policies, programmes and projects? Other issues that were on my mind were ways of enhancing media engagement with state actors on accountability, inefficient public financial management and corruption. It is when the role of the broadcast media become clearer and is well performed that Nigeria can free itself from poverty in the midst of plenty, now known in the development sector as "resource curse." The role of the media is anchored on the strong premise that information is development and development is information.

When Thomas Jefferson, the 3rd President of the United States, in 1787 said, "If I am to decide if I should have a government without the media or the media without a government, I will not hesitate to choose the latter," he was simply drawing national and international attention to the fact that the media is as important if not more important than government on issues of development. In the 21st century, the position of President Jefferson, over two centuries ago, has become even more topical, given the growing rate of poverty, inequality, illiteracy, ignorance and disease which have sharply divided the world into developed, developing and under-developed nations.

At the 6th Global Conference of the Extractive Industries Transparency Initiative, held in Sydney Australia in May 2013, development experts at the conference were also quick to identify access to information, competition, absence of sanctions and incentives among others, as the major issues that differentiate developing, under-developed and developed societies. The point, the experts argued, remains that issues of poor governance of resources common in most developing and under-developed nations; corruption, poor infrastructure, inadequate access to education, poor health care, lack of food and shelter and social insecurity among others, are functions of ignorance, arising from the inability of the citizens to have access to information required to make legitimate choices.

Many world leaders at that conference also explained that with unfettered access to information (which they contended is taken for granted in the developed world), the citizens will be in a position to initiate debate, dialogue, constructive engagement and discussions required to hold government in developing and under-developed countries accountable. Information is key in dealing with issues of development in poor and undeveloped nations; all attention should be directed at the broadcast media, which radio and television primarily represent.

This is more so because of the unique place of the broadcast media as the fastest, widest and most suitable way of reaching all categories of citizens, especially the ordinary citizens, who constitute the majority. Radio and television provide information to the people in the language they understand. They have the capacity to simplify the messages and deliver same in the most convenient pattern at little cost.

The Nigerian media in general and the broadcast media in particular have a responsibility in the areas of civic education on basic human liberty. The same goes for voter's education, governance, transparency, accountability, and ethical reorientation. The fact that sanctions and incentives, as earlier mentioned, appear to have become an exception rather than the norm, requires the broadcast media's intervention through deliberate focus on exposing corruption and unethical conducts.

Other areas of media focus include poor access to health care, increasing rate of mortality, unemployment, youth restiveness, and lack of basic infrastructure. There is also the need for the broadcast media to redirect attitude of governance towards production. But the broadcast media that I am part of in Nigeria is at the moment in no position to carry out these functions as a result of some institutional and man-made obstacles and challenges. The first challenge is the structure of ownership.

The ownership structure of the public-owned broadcast media in Nigeria which are actually in the majority have put the independence of the stations in question: Is it possible for he that pays the piper not to dictate the tune?

Many of these stations are dependent on government and thus have no power to assert editorial independence through news and programme content. Although commercialization and privatization policy to free these organisations from dependency have been proposed, implementation of the policy has not materialized over the years.

I must admit however, that government-owned media organisations can break away from the chains of self-censorship with a strong, professional and independent-minded leadership. Radio Nigeria experienced this between 1999 and 2005 when Eddie Iroh was Director General. Iroh's argument at that time remained that the first beneficiary of a credible public radio would be the government of the day. In his view, an independent public radio enjoys public confidence, trust and patronage in relation to its fair, objective and balanced output. It provides the government a larger platform to reach the people easily. But when government-owned media focuses only on government news and programmes, the listeners move away with their loyalty and patronage to stations with variety of news and diverse interests.

For the few private radio and television stations, their perceived independence is limited, as a result of the same reasons of ownership. Many of the owners of these organizations have their operations tied to whims and caprices of political elites. There is also the problem of survival in the rat-race for internally generated revenue in a society where economic activities are largely government dependent.

Other challenges include poor remuneration, industry exposure, training and manpower development. This is in addition to the inability of most of the stations, especially public-owned radio and television stations, to fully embrace digital broadcasting.

As I reflected on these and more challenges, I was inclined to support the conclusion of the lecturer that the time has come for us in Nigeria to do new things and to do them in completely different ways. There is ample evidence that the State can take measures to escape the resource curse. There are certain countries that have done so. They include Norway, Canada, Indonesia, Malaysia and Botswana. Nigeria too can emulate them.

For this to happen, the role of the media in liberating Nigeria from the syndrome of resource curse is the next challenge. A similar aggressive approach used by the media to send the military back to the barracks may be required in this next crucial but achievable challenge.

Chapter 14

The Digital "Switch-Over" Policy

During the greater period of my career in broadcasting, spanning almost three decades, the broadcasting industry in Nigeria and many developing countries operated largely with analogue, traditional, manual and obsolete equipment. Apart from the equipment, the orientation, environment and mind-set of the work force were also analogue-like.

Some of the broadcasting stations in Nigeria were so used to this traditional culture in both equipment, manpower and orientation that they appeared resistant to the emerging digital technology age. But Nigeria and other African countries are now experiencing a transition from analogue to digital technology broadcasting.

This followed the introduction of a "Switch-Over Policy" by the International Telecommunications Union (ITU). The policy was announced in 2006. Adeniyi (2009) asserts that the ITU's position on migration was informed by the development in telecommunication technologies. This development has enabled a more efficient use of radio frequency spectrum and improved quality picture and audio.

Until the development, the industry relied on radio spectrum for TV transmission with the inherent restriction posed by the analogue transmission. Adjacent analogue transmission were found to be subject to interference, forcing the regulatory bodies to leave spaces between channels and only allocate a small percentage of available spectrums for transmission, to ensure high quality transmission and reception throughout the regions served.

These entire disadvantages have been surpassed with the arrival of digitization, which gives better clarity and quality of signal and spectrum efficiency. Digitized TV signals in particular are clearer and stronger in their audio and video output.

Since digital technology has opened a world of possibilities for broadcasting, a huge spectrum will be available for radio and television broadcast in the country. As a result, more frequencies or wavelengths will be available for broadcasting as TV sets would now do much more than receive broadcast signals.

Under the global policy, all traditional, manual and analogue equipment in use in most broadcasting stations in sub-Saharan Africa will be phased out by January 15,

2015. In Nigeria, broadcasting organisations that would be affected mostly are government-owned radio and television stations. In most of the public-owned stations, the transmitting stations are still being manually operated, the consoles, recording panels, audio mixers, control room and studio equipment are largely analogue. Other areas to be affected by the digital switch-over policy are the use of cassettes, reel to reel tapes, and other manually operated studio consumables and services. Equally covered by the policy is the use of digital equipment for live transmissions and outside broadcast operations. But unknown to many, Radio Nigeria had led the digital way at the turn of the century when it began the establishment of 36 new FM stations spread across the 36 States of the federation. All the new stations and their full range of equipment were digital-compliant, ready for when the radio sets themselves would be digital.

Experts in the industry view the digitization policy deadline as a revolution and a technological innovation that will change the scope of radio and television broadcasting and expand the market with its infinite opportunities. By June 17, 2015, when the global switch-over is expected to come into effect, reception of analogue television, particularly by free to air transmission as is the case at the moment will no longer be possible.

To continue operating analogue broadcasting after this deadline would mean that Nigeria's signals would be impaired by signals from other countries. The implication therefore is that digital signals from neighbouring countries that meet the deadline will interfere with Nigeria's broadcasting and communication signals, thereby making it difficult to protect security and other sensitive broadcast messages. The switch-over policy is not a Nigerian phenomenon. It is a global policy being implemented in accordance with the Geneva Agreement signed by International Telecommunication Union (ITU) member countries in 2006.

Conceptualisation

The digitalisation policy is "a process, device or mechanism that operates by processing information supplied and stored in the form of a series of binary digits" (Robinson, 2004: p.373). Corroborating, Okpanachi (2008, p.4) says:

> *Digital radio is the pure digital transmission medium that improves the sound quality of radio broadcasts, virtually eliminating static, hiss, pops and fades and offers data display capabilities on receivers and opens up opportunity for multicasting: Broadcasting multiple high-quality channels on each frequency.*

Similarly, digitization of video signals, according to Baran (2010, p.227), "reduces their sizes and make it possible that more information can be carried over phone wires and stored." This view was advanced further by Hanson (2005, p.241):

> *Just as sound recording has moved to digital*

formats with CDs and MP3 files, so is television in the process of going from analogue technology of Farnsworth and Zworykin to the computerized digital technology. There are two distinct digital formats. High-definition television (HDTV) is a wide screen format and features an ultra-clear high resolution picture with superior sound... The other digital format is standard digital television, TV, which will make it possible to broadcast up to six channels on the same frequency space that now carries only one channel.

The quality of audio and visual signals in a digital technology framework is simply inviting to the audience in every positive way. It attracts interests and attention, conveying the very essence of information and communication technology in today's broadcasting. In the digital age, public interest patronage and awareness is on the increase towards high-definition television (HDTV) while the radio industry is introducing HD radio, a digital service that generally improves the signal quality of terrestrial radio stations. HD radio has the ability to enhance FM station to produce sound as good as CD. It can also make AM station sounds as good as current FM station. And the signals are static free. The notion here is that digital signals in broadcasting are superb. Rodman (2006, p.236) submits that:

Audience fragmentation has encouraged the development of digital radio which can increase format selections... In traditional analogue radio, an electronic waveform represents the sound on a carrier wave. Such a waveform carries static and is easily corrupted. In digital radio, transmitted sounds are assigned numbers (digits) that take up less air space than analogue waves... Digital signals can also result in crisp, clear signal.

From industry experience, the difference between traditional analogue broadcasting and digital broadcasting can be appreciated better when we compare AM and FM sound signal qualities. Besides, with digital technology, efficiency and professionalism is enhanced while human error, waste of time, energy and resources are reduced if not eliminated. Digitisation also helps the industry to maximise capacity utilisation, research and innovation. A digitised broadcasting house is in a better position to compete in an industry that has become globally market-driven and service-oriented. Developed nations like the United States, United Kingdom, France, Germany, Japan, Canada, etc., have since embraced digital broadcasting.

Against this background and in consideration of the obvious advantages of digital technology over analogue, the regulator of international telecommunications-ITU, conceptualised and evolved the policy of global switch-over. It also set the world deadline for compliance. Nigeria was a signatory to the global convention.

Nigeria's Response to Global Switch-Over Policy

In pursuance of the deadline to transit from analogue to digital, many nations covered by this convention designed policy measures to meet the deadline. Ocholi (2009, p.1), states that, "Nigeria officially started the digitization of its broadcast industry in December 2007 when President Yar'Adua gave approval." Following the approval, the digitization programme took off in Abuja on June 3, 2008 when the broadcasting community in Nigeria converged in the Federal Capital to discuss the implications of the policy for the industry and the economy and how the new policy would shape their respective field operations.

The outcome of the stakeholders dialogue led to the setting up of a Presidential Action Committee (PAC) to facilitate Nigeria's transition from analogue to digital broadcasting. The Committee came into effect on October 13, 2008 (Udeorah; 2009, p.7). It was the committee that set June 17, 2002 as switchover date in Nigeria. But as it were, the realisation of the Nigeria deadline was not to be.

The National Broadcasting Commission and the Broadcasting Organisations of Nigeria working with relevant government agencies and the private sector have come to accept the implementation of the policy in Nigeria as a huge challenge. The issue has dominated various meetings, seminars and workshops held recently within the broadcasting industry in the country. What has remained unclear is the way forward. As Special Assistant to a former Minister of Information and Communication, I was

211

familiar with the conversations and the issues involved in the demands for budgetary provisions and the realities to meet the challenges.

The Challenges

Implementation of the global switch-over policy to digital broadcasting in most developing countries, especially Nigeria, is fraught with several challenges. The first, according to Ekeh (2009, p. 2), lies with meeting the deadline of implementation of the actual migration from analogue to digital. This challenge arises out of the non-existence of policy structures and programmes that give the required confidence that the deadline would be met. These include challenges of stable power, frequent policy reversals, unstable political environment and poor infrastructure. As Ibulubo (2008, p. 1)asserted: "It is on record that NigComSat-1, the Nigeria Communication Satellite, launched into space in May 2007 was shut down in 2008 and not much has been done to revitalise the project that cost the country millions of dollars to implement'.'

Besides, there are technical capabilities required for the switch-over to happen. The technical manpower would need huge investments on the equipment and gadgets. At a time when government finances have been on a steady decline, the possibility that this aspect of the requirement would be met before the 2015 deadline is slim. Digital broadcast equipment which large broadcasting houses and networks like Nigerian Television Authority, NTA, Federal

Radio Corporation of Nigeria, FRCN, and the Voice of Nigeria, VON, require will cost billions of naira. The fate of State-owned radio and television stations in the thirty-six States of the Federation and the Federal Capital Territory with worse funding challenges also hang in the balance.

On the part of the audience, the ordinary listener with little or no digital compliant radio or television set, which will require some economic capacity to purchase, equally remain a huge challenge. As a result of poverty and low income profile of the average citizen, meeting the immediate demands of the change will not be easy.

There is also the problem of manpower to contend with in the desire to meet the deadline; the fragile but complex digital broadcast equipment requires trained manpower to manage them. But most broadcasting houses and organisations in Nigeria are lacking in this critical area.

Finally, there is obvious knowledge gap on what the policy on digital switch-over is and what it is not. The level of awareness is very low with scarcity of information in the public domain. As a result of poor literacy level, awareness creation over the policy is still a challenge. The National Broadcasting Commission, the Broadcasting Organisations of Nigeria and unions in the industry requires every support to meet this global deadline.

With music legend, King Sunny Ade

With NTA's Executive Director, Programmes, Eugenia Abu

With Eddie Iroh and Oby Ezekwesili

With Abubakar Jijiwa, Chairman, Broadcasting Organisation
of Nigeria and Director General, Voice of Nigeria

In an interview session with former INEC Chairman,
Dr. Abel Guobadiat

With Nuhu Ribadu at an event

Sharing jokes with Emeka Chikelu, former
Minister of Information

Justice Akanbi receiving a copy of Inside Aso Rock

Orji with his wife and children

Class of 2008 at Harvard Kennedy School
Orji sitting third from left in the first roll

Chapter 15

What We Never Learn in School

The experiences which I have attempted to share were from diverse industry exposure, driven by passion, responsibility, opportunities, risks and challenges while on the field. I did not learn them in the classroom. These experiences enabled me to see clearly the gap between theory and practice, digital and analogue, ancient and modern. They also exposed me to various environments as well as the barrier which an environment can pose to human aspirations.

From each encounter, I saw clearly the real issues in the practice of broadcasting in a developing country like Nigeria. These were issues and lessons outside what we learnt in school. But the lessons constitute what I may call influence mechanism and platform to seek the convergence of school and industry for any one hoping to make a successful career in the noble profession. I have attempted to outline and highlight some of the virtues and issues below.

Integrity

During a recent training at the Institute for Public and Private Partnership, Arlington Virginia, United States, a US security executive walked in to take the class on the topic: "Integrity: Anti-Corruption and Governance." The man, who should be in his early 60s, began the lecture with an open interaction on what integrity meant to governance and anti-corruption.

Those of us from Nigeria attending the programme dominated the interactive session on the subject with the confidence that we were in a familiar terrain. The debates on governance, corruption, or anti-corruption were topical issues in Nigeria before we left the country for the programme.

At that time, the oil subsidy probe scandal and similar governance issues seen as the bane of Nigeria's development were important topics in the public domain. The interactions at the programme revolved around the meaning of integrity, corruption, governance and public service and the links between integrity, anti-corruption and efficient service delivery. The lecturer also looked at the experiences of developed and developing nations with much of the examples coming from media reports on Nigeria.

But the most interesting and contentious part of the class discussion centred on if and how integrity can be transferred through teaching or learning to anyone seen or presumed to have none. The American instructor listened with rapt attention as the class of 34 participants, drawn mostly from Africa, Asia and the Caribbean, made spirited efforts to drive their points home. When the instructor was convinced that the participants had exhausted their energy trying to drive home their points on the subject matter, he called the class to order and then offered some insights and clarifications that indeed made a lot of impression on me.

The instructor began, "I retired a few years ago at the top echelon of the US Homeland Security. Let me inform all of you that you cannot teach anyone integrity. But you can teach anyone competence." He continued, "Integrity has a lot to do with character formation, the home, upbringing and genealogy," he concluded. At this point the class was calm as we all awaited a justification for his position. "You see," the instructor began to explain, "the major problem of you guys in Africa in particular is that you assign very sensitive and responsible positions to people whose character and conduct you have little or no knowledge of. But here in the United States, we carry out thorough investigations about whoever we want to assign the important responsibility of public trust. Our investigations are usually very deep, comprehensive and professional." He then added, "If the person's records are already available, then we cross check. The result of comprehensive security check on the individual will determine his suitability for the job, no matter how competent he is. We do not place as much emphasis on competence as we do on integrity because if integrity is alright, whatever gaps in the areas of competence can be addressed through training. But you cannot teach integrity. A thief is a thief." He warned the class, which was made up of senior management staff in public and private sector organisations that, "You don't need to place public interest at risk for the likelihood that the person would change while on the assignment."

The rest of us from Nigeria looked at each other and reflected on the process in our country; where many who appear for any kind of screening either compromise the process or are asked to simply take a bow and go. The instructor informed his now converted participants that the security checks and verifications begin from peer groups of the applicant within his neighbourhood to the person's behaviour in all the schools attended, police records, civic duties like payment of taxes, utility bills and related history. The investigations also cover employment history and community service profile. The person is eligible for the job for as long as no negative information related to integrity does surface. He explained that by this stringent policy but unavoidable process, people who know what they have done or failed to do with respect to integrity do not usually aspire to public office to avoid embarrassment. On the other hand, the process is a catalyst for all those who want a career in public service to embrace good conduct even at an early age.

I do not want to bore you with the definition of integrity because there are several of them, depending on the context and conceptualisation. Besides, integrity is one word that is very commonly used in Nigeria especially by those who abuse all that integrity represents on daily basis. They include politicians, businessmen and women, professionals and even religious leaders. In a country like Nigeria, many profess integrity but very few subscribe to its ideals. Integrity in this context, includes but is not limited to, virtues of discipline, honesty, diligence, trust, respect, responsibility and obedience to rules and regulations. It equally involves dependability, self-control, contentment and love. Broadcasting, from what I know, is an integrity driven profession, built strongly on professional discipline, morals and good ethical conducts.

From the institutional standpoint, there is a commonly shared view that both the content of news and programmes from any radio or television station must reflect professional integrity. These include upholding the sanctity of truth, fairness, balance and objectivity as an ethical business operational model. It includes such other minor but very important issues like regular "time-checks and time-keeping", prompt response to listeners' concerns, staff issues and corporate social responsibility. Time regulates every broadcasting activity, news and programmes inclusive.

For the broadcaster, integrity is everything, especially in dealing with the listeners and the public in order to sustain trust and confidence. A broadcaster therefore should be one who is honest sincere and trusted. Anything in the contrary affects the message and credibility of the station which eventually leads to loss of public confidence.

Loyalty

I am not too sure if loyalty can be taught in school as a subject. Loyalty sounds to me like a virtue, a culture or attitude which can be cultivated, nurtured and internalised. It is also closely aligned with integrity. However, for loyalty to firmly manifest, there must be patience, contentment, honesty and discipline. In broadcasting, loyalty is a salient critical success factor for professional career growth. Loyalty in this context, is the ability of a staff to believe strongly in the future and prospects of the media organisation he/she represents. In broadcasting, where there is a high rate of labour mobility and transition, especially after the deregulation of the industry, the issue of loyalty becomes imperative.

Many broadcasters move from one organisation to another with the excuse of searching for the so-called greener pastures with little or no recourse to institutional loyalty. On the other hand, there are radio and television stations that do nothing to recognise or reward staff loyalty. But loyalty is a factor we need to consider as fundamental. The argument that a patient dog eats no bone in Nigeria should be discouraged. During my career, I have seen several examples, where a patient dog actually ate the fattest meat, not bone. This occured as a result of our loyalty to an organisation that offered us platform to become celebrities. Only field experience can present the circumstances and the choices. It is beyond the classroom.

Initiative

Another attribute that is not learnt in the classroom is initiative. In this context, initiative is the ability, resilience and capability to squeeze water out of rock. It is also the rare drive, penetration and talent to create something out of nothing. Some also view initiative as not just the zeal to succeed where many have failed but the tendency to produce results instead of reasons.

A reporter sent to cover an assignment will face the wrath of the editor if he returns to the news room without a story. If the event did not hold, initiative requires that the reporter find out why and what was responsible for the cancellation. Are they political, economic or social management obstacles or are there controversial reasons for the cancellation?

Are there damages or possible consequences of the failure of the event to hold? What is the next step after the cancellation and who is responsible for taking the step? In an attempt to provide these answers, the reporter will be in a position to build a very good story, capable of setting a new agenda. In some cases, a story built under this circumstance impresses the editor more than if the event held. But it requires initiative to turn challenges into opportunities in broadcasting. I have just one similar experience to share. I was in the Federal Government Presidential delegation for the swearing-in of Nelson

Mandela as first black President of South Africa. The event was held in South Africa on May 10, 1994 shortly after the first multi-racial election.

General Sani Abacha, the then Head of State led the Nigerian delegation made up of two former Heads of States and a large contingent of Nigerian officials, diplomats and businessmen. As one of the frontline states in the anti-apartheid struggle, Nigeria's participation meant so much to South Africa. It was also an assignment to which media organisations were expected to send very experienced reporters.

I recall that out of the six Nigerian journalists that were in that global event, I was certainly the youngest and least experienced. The list included Kayode Soyinka, then London Bureau Chief of Newswatch magazine, Chris Anyanwu (now a Senator), then Publisher of TSM (the Sunday Magazine) and Chris Ngwu, a Controller of News and NTA State House Correspondent. Others were Isa Hussein of News Agency of Nigeria and Yemi Fakayeijor of Voice of Nigeria. At that time, I was just a young graduate reporter on Grade level 09.

Thus, I had to justify my suitability to be sent to such high profile event, given my limited exposure to international assignments. For me, only results not reasons were good enough, at least to vindicate those who gave me the opportunity in spite of sceptics. I therefore arrived in South Africa, desperate and determined. In the programme for the ceremony, the first major event was the inauguration of South African Parliament. At the inaugural session,

Mandela would be formally elected and endorsed as the President-elect. And this important aspect of the event had to hold a day before the Presidential Swearing-in (May 9th, 1994). South Africa was operating a parliamentary system.

In South Africa, while the seat of government is in the capital, Pretoria, the parliament is located in the commercial mining city of Cape Town. From Pretoria to Cape Town is about two and half hours by air, almost twice any air travel time within Nigeria. As a result, the organisers have arranged an aircraft to fly heads of delegations that were in Pretoria (where the Presidential inauguration would hold) to Cape Town to witness the inauguration. The aircraft provided had no room for the world press corps that were covering the event. As a result, all of us in the press team were stranded, while the VIPs leading the delegation took off and left the media team behind.

I was deeply depressed and frustrated on what to tell the people at the newsroom in Ikoyi, Lagos who had left a dedicated telephone line open in expectation of my reports. As all the stranded reporters dispersed, I thought hard about how to get out of the situation I found myself in.

At the entrance of the hotel, Carlton Johannesburg, I saw a newspaper stand and bought a local newspaper. The newspaper contained a comprehensive story and analysis of the Cape Town Parliamentary inauguration I was just about to miss. The story analysed in great detail the composition of the parliament. It outlined the contentious issues over Mandela's expected emergence as President-elect, issues on the rivalry between Mandela's African

National Congress (ANC) and the opposition, especially the IN Katha Freedom Party led then by Chief Mangasutu Buthelezi.

The local newspaper I had in my hand took me into the minds of the average black South African and made me understand the expectations at the inauguration and other local issues which the listeners not present in South Africa would be interested to hear from me. And as I was trying to savour the relief which the information in the newspaper had provided, I entered my hotel room, turned the television and saw the event being broadcast live by the South African Broadcasting Corporation (SABC TV). The CNN was also covering the event for the international audience but the SABC coverage was more detailed and interesting for the African audience.

At that time, CNN was the exclusive preserve of a small elite in Nigeria which included newsrooms, unlike now. With this opportunity that was created by initiative, I relaxed in my hotel room, put my recorder by the television set, recorded important speeches and developed my story with insights from the comprehensive information which the local newspaper provided. At 4p.m on May 9, 1994, I was able to satisfy the editor, the newsroom and listeners nationwide in spite of obstacles. It would have been disastrous to fail on that duty. No one except me would have believed my story.

Newsroom Politics

The politics in every newsroom is real and cannot be ignored. It revolves around who gets what, how, where, why and when? The politics cuts across the rank and file, management as well as the staff in every broadcasting house. Except a broadcaster understands the politics in the newsroom, mere dependence on merit, efficiency, hardwork and results may not be enough. Newsroom politics sometimes influences staff deployment, appointments and privileges. This includes favourable schedule of duties, training opportunities, beat postings and assignments. Understanding the politics is not a classroom thing; it is a field experience that one must be ready to contend with. It is also not limited to Nigeria, what may differ is the approach. To understand the politics and benefit from it, one needs to embrace humility, team spirit and sportsmanship.

Besides, luck, availability, visibility and friendship with all will help. This is in addition to trust, reliability, efficiency in all assigned duties and commitment to results. In all my years at the Broadcasting House, I met and managed the challenges of Newsroom politics with great caution and wisdom. But to pretend that it doesn't exist is an illusion.

Structure

A broadcaster or broadcasting organisation needs a structure for effective field operation. If one exists, it needs to be regularly serviced but if none exists, please establish one. The structure syndrome has become a phenomenal factor to succeed in broadcasting. Politicians in Nigeria understand the importance of structure more than anyone else. In the context of politics, existence of structure simply refers to various organs or levels of support that a politician has built over the years in order to sustain the grassroot appeal to his/her aspirations.

But in broadcasting, it represents levels of important contacts that drive one's growth and performance in assigned duties. This includes the silent but effective contacts at various levels in the organisation, outside the organisation, in the public and among colleagues. The structure consist of the database of these contacts which is effectively put into use to accomplish complex tasks that put one miles ahead of others. Structure is also fundamental for career growth and development. With a structure, the effect of newsroom politics will be positive. However, every structure needs to be serviced regularly like a car. How it works in a broadcasting house is a story for another day.

Societal Patronage

They are many broadcasters who lack societal patronage because they are only heard but not seen. In my days at the broadcasting house, we had excellent broadcasters who were "tigers" in-house but were nobody as such outside the broadcasting house because they were so withdrawn or disconnected from the society. We use to call the senior ones, "studio elephants" and the junior ones, "studio rats". These are very popular voices we hear daily on radio and faces we see on television but the society has no access to interact with them. This class of broadcasters are too closely married to the job schedules that they do nothing else. Even when they are off duty, they have nowhere else to go but the broadcasting house. They fail to create any viable legitimate platform to engage the public in a manner that sells their original personality outside the studio. The society therefore has no opportunity to access and explore their other potential and offer them legitimate patronage.

The broadcasters in this category are shy and introverted; they hardly attend public functions or organise one. In circumstances where they do attend, they appear conscious of their studio personality in a manner that puts the public off. The public perceive them either rightly or wrongly as arrogant or people with inferiority or superiority complex. Many in this category remain poor because their other potential are hardly known, or utilised.

I never knew all these until a close friend, Dan dragged me to Peak Nite Club at the heart of Surulere one fateful night. As soon as I was introduced, I was shocked by the attention my name attracted. Many listeners familiar with my reports and programmes on radio clustered around me and exchanged pleasantries. I also got contacts that night that offered me useful and beneficial exposure in Lagos.

From that night, the contacts ensured that no weekend in Lagos was a waste. On weekends, we moved from Peak Nite Club in Surulere, Lagos, to Kolex Nite Club somewhere in Yaba, to the Lords in Maryland, Nite Shift, off Toyin Street, Ikeja and end up at Stadium Hotel where Sir Victor Olaiya ends the night with his pre-independence and irresistible High Life music. On other weekends, we chose the African Shrine which was also in Ikeja and watched Fela Anikulapo Kuti play. This was between 1989 to 1992.

During that period, Lagos hardly sleept on weekends. We moved freely from the Island, where I lived, to the Mainland which was even more bubbly. It was real Lagos life for *Lagosians* who knew where to go. Besides, Lagos was peaceful and quite secure at that time. For some, it was sports that occupied their evenings. They joined such elites clubs like Ikoyi Club, Lagos Island Club, etc. The contacts and exposure from social gatherings can be of immense benefit. From my diverse experience, success in broadcasting depends on how you explore the society and share in its infinite opportunities and not just on being a slave to the microphone and the studios. This again is beyond the classroom.

Chapter 16

Behind the Issues and Matters Arising

The experiences I have shared over the previous chapters largely represent a transition from ancient to modern and analogue to digital technology as the media broadcast industry, especially public-owned radio and television stations in Nigeria, face the challenges of a new democratic society in an industry that has become globally competitive. Jeffrey Sachs warned in his book, "Common Wealth" that time has come for all nations and institutions to face squarely a new development strategy and economic paradigm that is globally inclusive, cooperative, open, transparent, environmentally aware, and science-based. Sachs further warned that all nations and public institutions are running against a crowded planet. The option available to nations and institutions is to get rid of all threats to their respective global wellbeing; all of which are solvable but potentially disastrous if left unattended."

In his view, "prosperity must be maintained through new strategies for sustainable development that complements market forces, spread sustainable technologies, stabilize global population and enable billions of the poorest of the poor people escape from the trap of extreme poverty." The issues of increasing mass poverty, impunity in corrupt practices, environmental degradation, explosion in population growth, decline in public health, and access to quality education, Sachs warned, have become key determinants of war and peace. He contended that the very idea of nations scrambling for power, natural resources, and markets must give way to a new era of global cooperation around shared goals of promoting sustainable development. He underlined the need for global attention to basic freedoms, rule of law, good governance and competition.

I therefore think that now that capacity to deliver prosperity to the greatest number of Nigerians has come with a return to civil rule, the role of the media, especially the publicly owned media, needs to change to deeply reflect more democratic values and principles in the content and quality of news and programmes.

The warning by Jeff Sachs resonates when one takes a look at the challenges facing the government-owned media organizations such as radio and television stations. Apart from problems of funding, poor facilities, poor remunerations, self and institutional censorship, many, if not all, still operate with mindsets, psychology and business modules of monopoly. From industry experience in the sector, I think very strongly that the time for massive institutional and structural reforms in public broadcast media organizations has become more urgent.

The broadcast media reforms will put these organizations in a better position to deepen the nation's democracy, compete in the industry and reduce their dependence on government for virtually everything. The reforms will also re-position the broadcast media to play leading roles in development issues raised by Jeff Sachs in his book, many of which Nigeria has to contend with.

The history of the BBC, VOA, Radio Deutsche Welle, Radio India, and South Africa's SABC are replete with similar examples. Each of these big and strong radio networks mentioned function effectively in these big democratic nations with very little or no dependence on government. I was at the Thompson Foundation Institute for Advanced Media Studies, Cardiff United Kingdom between April 21st and 21st October 1995 on Commonwealth Fellowship training on broadcasting and time-based media. Broadcasters from India, South Africa and Namibia were among those in attendance. At that time, South Africa was about a year post-Apartheid, following the inauguration of Nelson Mandela as the first democratic President on May 10, 1994. Part of the training was a review of the structures of public media organizations.

My excuse to the class, made up of broadcasters from 18 countries, was that the structure we have was because my country was under military rule. But I was surprised that just one year after Apartheid, the South African Broadcasting Corporation (SABC) had commenced reforms to re-position the organization for a new role under a democracy. The story of series of reforms that took place in Radio India is as old as that country's independence. After 29 years of military rule and 13 years of democracy, the time to reform public radio and television stations in Nigeria is long overdue.

I am certain that if reforms are being pursued vigorously in such sensitive sectors in Nigeria like telecommunications, public procurement, power, banking, extractive industry, among others, that of the broadcast media will even be more interesting and beneficial, given the important role of radio and television in a democracy, governance and development.

Another area of concern is in training, capacity building and manpower development. Traditionally, the average citizen believes with every confidence that whatever is said or announced on radio and seen on television with respect to news and programmes are the truth and nothing but the truth. The founding fathers of broadcasting in Nigeria from the era of Nigeria Broadcasting Service (NBS), to the period of Nigeria Broadcasting Corporation (NBC), to the present day Federal Radio Corporation of Nigeria (FRCN), the Nigerian Television Authority (NTA) and the Voice of Nigeria (VOA), did put in place specific policies and tradition to ensure the sustenance of this public confidence. It is worthy of note that nearly all State-owned radio and television stations in Nigeria, including NTA and VON, are in one way or the other the offshoot of old NBC. NTA was NBC-Television and VON was the External Broadcasting Service of NBC, where literary icons like the late Chinua Achebe cut their teeth.

So, one way the founding fathers sustained the confidence and tradition was through exposure of all cadres of staff to training and capacity building. Hence the establishment of the FRCN Staff Training School in Sogunle, Lagos and the Television College in Jos. These two institutions represent in the broadcasting industry, what the Nigerian Defense Academy represents for military officers in the Nigerian Armed Forces. The FRCN training School in Sogunle and the TV College, Jos, were also the only ones in West Africa.

They received students from broadcast media organizations in West Africa and beyond. Attendance, participation and successful certification in designated training programmes by either Sogunle or Jos were strict conditions for promotion and career advancement in the industry at that time. All broadcasters of repute that I know attended either of these training schools or both. In my career, I attended the Radio Nigeria Training School at least three times, spending a minimum of two months in the school for each training programme.

I have not visited the school for a long time now and therefore not in a position to comment on the state of facilities in the school at the moment but during our time, all basic facilities were in place and well maintained. These included the studio clinics, hostels, classrooms, teaching aids, school canteen, etc. The resource persons were also drawn from diverse areas of the industry.

I remember tough trainings in the school, under such instructors like Stella Awani, Marrie Irekefe, Joseph Angulu, Adedun Ogunleye, Lawrence Emeka, Biodun Sotunbi, Andy Anarado, etc. The training covered techniques in news sourcing, development and writing, programme presentation, pronunciation, programme production, radio engineering management, studio management, administration and finance, etc. The trainings were so rigorous that broadcasters were drilled on such minute details like pronunciation of Nigerian names and peculiar English words. Through the emphasis on training and re-training of all categories of staff in the broadcasting industry, we were groomed into internalizing the fact that a mistake on air was a taboo. Those who committed the taboo faced severe sanctions; some of them got frustrated and left the profession.

Also compulsory was the use of written, edited and certified scripts before one goes on air, arrival on time for the programme so as to go through thorough rehearsals. One also has to have the passion and humility to ask questions when in doubt. For the news unit, editors and reporters functioned strictly on known media slogan – "Facts are sacred, opinion is free." Due to these trainings we had, it was very rare to hear "I am sorry" on air, or hear or see presenters coughing anyhow while on air, poor grammar on air or careless and vulgar statements that offend the sensibility of listeners.

Common mistakes we find in the media today include the "murder" of Nigerian names and English words, illogical arguments that make no sense to the listeners, poor alignment of music to the programme and uncoordinated airing of adverts during programmes. These and more factors have led to loss of confidence in the industry.

Beyond these issues, it is doubtful if there is any other profession that uplifts the people and unites the nation like broadcasting. This perhaps explains the reason why FRCN has continued to operate to the best of its ability on this vision and mission, despite the challenges. I do not need to bore anyone with the importance of radio and television in a developing nation like Nigeria.

It is also important to point out that the emergence of the new media cannot be an alternative to radio and television. At the recent General Assembly of the Broadcasting Organization of Nigeria (BON) held at the Premier Hotel, Ibadan which I attended as one of the resource persons, I listened attentively to an impressive presentation by the former Chairman of the Nigeria Broadcasting Commission, Biodun Bolarinwa. His presentation at that forum, attended by Chief Executives of radio and television stations in Nigeria, centered on building a convergence between old and new media. I am persuaded by that presentation to believe that it is the right way to go. The new media, as already highlighted in this book, has its own advantages and disadvantages like the traditional media. What needs to be done to save the society from information disorder and dislocation is a compromise based on what Bolarinwa called convergence. Many countries have already developed strategies to respond to this development.

During my career spanning about three decades, I assumed that the broadcasting industry with its depth of exposure to knowledge, information and entertainment, emerging opportunities in technology, and expansion of democratic institutions would help eliminate the common regime of brown or white envelope journalism. I therefore decided to begin early enough to devote more energy to self-development through expansion of knowledge and education in other areas outside the profession.

But the economic conditions in our country has brought about deep frustration in the industry, resulting in a deterioration of basic ethical conducts in the discharge of our duties. At the root of the programmes of the broadcast industry is moral crisis: lack of civic virtue, contentment, dignity of labour and passion for public interest. It is common for us to openly condemn economic and political leaders on issues of corruption in our stations but fail to behave with respect, honesty, and dignity at private and public functions in open pursuit of brown, black, white, red or green envelopes. As broadcasters, our names and faces attract instant attention. This is a big burden with the huge responsibility of protecting our image, the image of the profession and the station we represent.

We need to be conscious of our image and watch our attitude in private and public places of assignment. We ought to reflect "our industry imposed personality" and role model status, by showing acts of good citizenship, educating ourselves promptly on public issues and acting in favour of the needs of the society, and be consciously aware of our role as agents of change and development in society.

Against this background and in the light of experiences shared in this book, anyone who wants to make a career in broadcasting has to embrace an early culture of learning, education and self-development even in the face of poor remuneration. You may recall the story of our encounter with the landlord where three well-known broadcasters (although at the local level) were unable to pay the monthly house rent of One hundred and twenty naira only (₦120). As Will Daurent wrote: "Sixty years ago, I know everything, today, I know nothing." Education is a progressive discovery of man's ignorance. The Unity University of Nigeria in its motto, made it simpler: "To restore the dignity of Man." The importance of education in broadcasting cannot be overemphasized.

The other advice to the young and upcoming broadcasters who are determined to make a career in the profession is that day cultivate the culture of patience, resilience, penetration, passion and drive even in difficult situations. Sometimes, you find yourself working under a tough boss that neither appreciates your worth, work, commitment, plan nor is interested in your growth. Please do not give up. We all had those challenges. But many of us refused to take the easy options. As President Barrack Obama told the American people in his State of the Union address of January 28th, 2014, "nothing in life that is worth something comes easy." From my years of industry experience, a broadcaster is not defined by limits but by potential. What is very important is not how you started but how you finished. Like Ralph Opara, a renowned broadcaster, will always say when you seek his advice durng trials, "This too will come and pass."

To drive this message home, whenever I travel by road, I keep myself busy by reading   funny but insightful messages on the usually over-loaded big lorries popularly known in Igbo as *gwongworo*. Such messages include, "Let my enemy be alive and see what I will be in future"; "The downfall of a man is not the end of his life"; "Six persons! No standing"; "Horn before overtaking"; "Who knows tomorrow?" And the one I love most that makes me reel with laughter, "Lagos is a school, Iddo is my class." Please note that origin of this wise counsels is mostly from motor parks filled with lorry drivers, touts and mechanics with little or no access to good education.

One other fundamental suggestion is a comprehensive review of the processes, procedures and conditions for issuance of broadcasting licenses in Nigeria. The comprehensive review, which should form part of the broadcast media reforms, will help to restore the broadcast industry back to its rightful owners. Under the current arrangement, a broadcaster with all the required experience, take-off capital and industry exposure will be unable to obtain a license to establish a radio or television license. The procedure, as it is now, has placed the industry in the hands of middlemen, quacks and greedy investors resulting in far-reaching negative consequences on professionalism.

The time has also come for our country to embrace the policy on community radio. The community radio concept is geared towards bridging rural-urban information gap which is currently huge in Nigeria and most developing nations.

The community radio concept is aimed at providing grassroot based alternative platform for audiences in rural and remote communities so they can have information on issues and events delivered in their local languages and context. The target audience is the low income groups, rural farmers, market men and women, traditional rulers, town unions, rural-based age grades, etc. Therefore, the introduction of community radio in Nigeria will help boost rural development through bridging the gap in rural information dissemination.

Chapter 17

Travel Log

One of the privileges that broadcasters and media professionals enjoy in Nigeria and developing countries is exposure to local and international travels. The job has the potential to take one to any part of the country and beyond, sometimes without notice.

These trips expose the broadcaster to other cultures, customs and traditions as well as levels of development. In Nigeria and most developing countries, where the condition of service in the industry can hardly guarantee independent funding of the trips, the media often rely on government support and other forms of sponsorships to make these trips. The merits and demerits of this government sponsorship arrangement in terms of independence of the reporter, credibility of the reports and fairness and balance is an issue for another book.

But for now, I must confess that I benefitted enormously from this existing culture of sponsorships to cover assignments at both the local and international arena. In Nigeria, the job took me to towns and villages that I never imagined existed. I have travelled from Abuja by road through Keffi to Jos, passing through Bauchi, Katagum, Damaturu through Maiduguri to Biu, an ancient district in Borno state. Biu is less than an hour's drive to Cameroun but about two hours' drive to Maiduguri. What about a 4-hour trip on speed boat from Port Harcourt to Nembe? From Bauchi, through Gombe passing through Numan to Yola down to Taraba, the traveller is in direct contact with nature; arable agricultural basins buried within flourishing hills and valleys, and enjoying the sweet breeze from the Mambilla Plateau.

From Kaduna, passing through Gusau, through Sokoto to Kebbi, Yauri or Argungu, the traveller is exposed to nature with men and camels providing incredible workforce in support of massive traditional farming driven by irrigation. One of the fascinating trips I made in that axis was a trip through Katsina to Jirbia, a border town between Nigeria and Niger Republic. In Jirbia, cross-border trades in textiles, hides and skins and fuel products are common. A trip from Abuja through Benue, Obudu, Ikom to Calabar, through Uyo, Eket to Port Harcourt, passing through Ikwere land by Imo river through Ngor Okpalla to Owerri, Ngbidi, Ihiala, Okija through Onitsha, Agbor, Uromi to Okene, Lokoja to Abuja exposes one to our country's diverse cultures and traditions.

242

While covering the Ife - Modakeke crisis of 1995, I came to appreciate the fact that Ife and Modakeke were like two young men sharing a two-bedroom flat. There is no boundary that I saw between them. What I saw was a shocking discovery that Ife and Modakeke were like twins. From Ife to Ilesha, Ede, Oshogbo to Ibadan up to Ogbomosho, the traveller is in contact with history expressed in sculptors, arts and western education. The people are knowledgeable, deeply rooted in morals, with a tough communal resistance to oppression. This exposure matters in all ramifications to a broadcaster in order to see how far our voices go and to see the cultures we strive to influence through our news and programmes.

While I was in the field, I was privileged to have travelled round Nigeria, all the 15 member countries of ECOWAS, all prominent countries in Africa and across the world. I cannot remember any popular country in the world that media assignments have not taken me to except Russia and Brazil. Here are some countries I have been to: USA, Britain, France, Germany, Netherlands, Denmark, India, Indonesia, Jordan, Saudi Arabia, Jamaica, South Africa, Tunisia, Egypt, Morocco, Turkey, South Korea, North Korea, China, Libya, Japan, Ethiopia, Thailand, Switzerland, Norway, Peru, Tanzania, and Australia.

The point here is that for a broadcaster, travelling is indeed education, not part of it. I made some of the trips either as a reporter, correspondent, editor or as part of media relations duties. Each trip has its own peculiar story. It is always important for a reporter to keep a diary. This can make an interesting read. Below is a recent log I would like to share:

MEMORIES OF SYDNEY!

A trip to Sydney, I was told, is a journey to the end of the world. From any part of the world and by whichever means, travelling to Sydney, the biggest city in Australia is certainly a journey and an experience to treasure. Many look forward to visiting Sydney at least once in a lifetime because of what the city represents in tourism, business, culture and global development.

On May 18, 2013, I had this rare privilege and looked forward to the trip with all excitement and expectations. The event was the 6th Global Conference of the Extractive Industries Transparency Initiative; a meeting point for delegates from over fifty member countries to converge, exchange ideas, compare notes and set new agenda on the way forward for the world body.

The Sydney Conference with the theme "transparency counts" attracted over 1200 delegates from 96 countries. Delegates were drawn from government representatives, media/civil society, legislature, companies, investors, development partners, the diplomatic community and others with varied interests in extractive industries from all parts of the world.

The journey began on Emirate Airlines on a 7-hour flight from Lagos to Dubai. Since the Lagos–Dubai flight was all through the night, I had a sound sleep, woke up to embrace the lovely Dubai Airport where truly and indeed the world connects. At Dubai Airport, every passenger, visitor or traveler feels important. No matter how often one lands at that airport, (an architectural masterpiece anyday day), everything appears new and inviting, making each second one spends or money expended worth it.

From Dubai airport, the journey to Sydney just began with 15 more hours to go. In my case, I was connecting through Bangkok, Thailand, a distance of 5 to 6 hours from Dubai. The journey to Bangkok seemed the longest ever. I was awake all through and I had a seat next to someone who could neither speak nor understand English. Efforts to engage my neighbor in a discussion met a brick wall, compelling me to read Nasiru El Rufai's book - *Accidental Public Servant,* which, luckily, I took along with me.

Throughout the duration of that flight, I was glued to El Rufai's book which consists of engaging stories about his background, experiences in school, in the private sector, how he got into public office, what he did or failed to do at the Bureau of Public Enterprises, as Minister of Abuja and his "battles" with his fellow ruling political elites. I took particular interest in El Rufai's stories on the PDTF scandals, his allegations of bribery and corruption against Senator Ibrahim Mantu and his testimony at the National Assembly over his tenure as FCT Minister as well as other issues where he was at the center of controversy.

I considered some lessons from El Rufai's stories in that book an important part of my memories of Sydney. Some of the lessons made a lot of impressions on me during and after the trip. First was the need to take bold, daring, final and deterrent decisions on any problem that continues to reoccur and constitute "a terror" in our daily lives. According to El Rufai in his book, that will put a stop to such a problem once and for all.

In that book, El Rufai told a story of a certain school mate (Sunday) in his secondary school, Barewa College, who bullied him at will because of his size. His story was on the far-reaching measures he took to respond adequately and ensured that the aggressor left him alone. In our daily lives, we have people who constitute terror in our lives with their failures and problems and we keep tolerating their distractions and unending demands, resulting in what economists call "shifting targets". One other interesting part of the book was a personal conversation between El Rufai and President Obasanjo over El Rufai's decision to resign his appointment as Director General of Bureau of Public Enterprises, BPE.

According to El Rufai, when he took his letter of resignation to the President, citing undue pressure in carrying out his duties as an excuse, Obasanjo locked his office and this candid conversation followed. "Well, my short friend, I am not going to discuss any resignation and I am not going to redeploy you." President Obasanjo began, "You know why? I am the father of everyone here and I have a duty to train you. I have a duty to make sure you learn to work with everyone, not just people you like. In public service, you meet people you do not like and you must learn to work with them. This is not your company where you choose who you work with, this is the government of Nigeria and everyone, good or bad, has equal rights to be part of it."

At this point, El Rufai interrupted, "But Mr President, why learn to work with people I don't like?" " Because you see," Obasanjo continued, "you are a good man, a clever man. One day, if you play your cards right, you will do even greater things in government than you are doing today, so I have a duty to develop you, smoothen your rough edges and reduce the obstacles you will face in future public life." Obasanjo cleared his throat as El Rufai and his friend, Steve Oronsaye, who accompanied him to see the President, listened with rapt attention.

"Listen, let me tell you," Obasanjo continued, "You know you have three problems. Each one of the problems is enough of a problem by itself, but you have all three. Your first problem is that you are very clever. People generally do not like clever people. You are clever. That alone attracts enemies. Your second problem is that you look clever and that is a bigger problem." Obasanjo added. " Your third problem is that you speak clever, you act clever, you are impatient with people who are not as smart as you are, you talk down to them. That is why people will not like you." Obasanjo summed up. "But look at me," President Obasanjo drew El Rufai's attention to himself, "In my time, I was not as smart as you are. I have gone through your grades in school. You got A's in high school; A's in A levels and first class honours. I did not go to the University but I took my high school graduation exams a year in advance and I got A's, so I was also clever in school. But I am lucky; God gave me a not-so-clever face. People look at me and think I am stupid. You can't look at me and know what is going on in my brain. You know what I do?" Obasanjo asked El Rufai. "I behave like a bushman. See what that has done to me. I am here as Nigeria's President. Far smarter people than me are out there. There is nothing you can do about your face, but you can reduce the enemies you have by avoiding the problem of being too clever.' Obasanjo admonished El Rufai.

These and many more wise counsels conveyed in very high profile conversations made me to appreciate that book as a worthy companion suited for such a long trip. On arriving at Bangkok, 7 hours after, already tired and exhausted, I wondered where the strength to sit down in another plane for another 9 hours to Sydney will come from.

With these thoughts in my head, we changed flights from Emirates to Qantas Airline en route Sydney. The journey turned out to be quite exciting. The person sitting next to me was quite versatile in world affairs and had spent considerable time in Nigeria, Tanzania and Uganda. We engaged each other in various discussions until we dozed off.

On arrival at Sydney Australia, I met a civilized and developed society where what seemed to matter most was discipline, driven by contentment and courtesy to the next person. From the airport, everyone I met, even the lawns, grasses and trees, appeared happy and at peace with themselves. As we drove from the airport to the town, a first time visitor is ushered into a city with beautiful harbor, parks, a stunning coastline, amazing water fronts and historic buildings that will delight tourists.

Besides, the city has well-developed infrastructure. And this is obvious by the roads and streets. In the words of Clover Moore, the Lord Mayor of Sydney. "Our harbor city Sydney is Australia's face to the world, and the world's portal to Australia. It is a vibrant, eclectic, hospitable and beautiful place that Sydneysiders are proud to call home and the almost three million visitors a year delight in discovering." I took this message seriously and began to plot how to explore Sydney, as we made steady progress on our leisure drive from the Sydney International Airport to the town. I am glad I did. The rest, as the saying goes, is a story for another day.

The weeklong global conference held at the famous Sydney International Exhibition and Convention Centre located in Sydney's tourists haven, Darling Harbour, near the central business district. Opened in 1998, the venue was part of the edifice used for the Sydney 2000 Olympics Games. The venue is a tourist attraction by every standards.

The conference began with regional meetings of implementing countries from the AngloGold Ashanti bloc, Francophone Africa and the EITI Latin America respectively. Each of these meetings appraised their implementation problems and prospects in their respective countries. It was also an opportunity to plot how to engage the West and developed nations to support the EITI process for the political economy and social dynamics surrounding the EITI as a multi-stakeholder driven social movement. The opening of the conference was attended by world leaders in government, business and development from poor and rich nations.

Nigeria's Minister of Mines and Steel Development, Musa Mohammed Sada, led Nigeria's delegation to the event, supported by the chairman and representatives of Nigeria Extractive Industries Transparency Initiative (NEITI) National Stakeholders Working Group. Many decisions were taken; one of them was how the EITI process can lead to positive change and improved quality of life for citizens of resource-rich nations. To achieve this, the global conference witnessed the launching of revised Extractive Industries Transparency Initiative EITI standards.

More countries such as the United States, France, United Kingdom and host country, Australia, confirmed their intention to join the EITI as implementing countries. By Day 4 of the conference, the Nigerian camp in Sydney was already looking forward to going home and was in need of local food. At the intervention of Nigerian Embassy officials, the services of a Nigerian caterer based in Sydney was procured to prepare special Nigerian dishes for the team so as to dilute the western food that have got many sick.

I took the initiative to interview the caterer to ascertain her competence and track record for this important assignment. Before I could begin, the woman took over the interview with a long history of her track records in cooking for the high and mighty who had visited Australia from

Nigeria and indeed Africa, in the past. She boasted that her food is better than that of any good caterer in Abuja, Lagos or Calabar and challenged me to give it a trial. With this assurance, the service of the "expert" was procured.

I took the liberty to make announcements to all; that they should look forward to the food. Expectations were high among the delegates. I received several calls in my room demanding to know when the food was arriving. Many missed their normal meals in the hotel. I made passionate appeals for them to be patient, with every reassurance that the meal would be worth the effort. But as it were, the caterer eventually arrived with the food and it was a disaster. The woman must have used a full bag of salt to prepare the food!

Appendices

LIST OF MAJOR RADIO AND TELEVISION STATIONS IN NIGERIA

FEDERAL RADIO CORPORATION OF NIGERIA

S/N	NAME OF RADIO STATION	ADDRESS	BROADCASTING FREQUENCY
1.	FRCN Network	Radio House, Area 8, Garki, Abuja.	
2.	Radio Nigeria, Abuja National Station	Broadcasting House, Gwagwalada, Abuja.	
3.	Radio Nigeria, Lagos	Broadcasting House, Ikoyi, Lagos.	
4.	Radio Nigeria, Enugu	Broadcasting House, No. 7, Onitsha Road, Enugu.	
5.	Radio Nigeria, Kaduna	No.7, Yakubu Gowon Way, Kaduna.	
6.	Radio Nigeria, Ibadan	Broadcasting House, No. 1 Oba Adebimpe Road, Ibadan, Oyo State.	
7.	FRCN Training Institution	Adekunle Fajuyi Road, GRA, Ikeja, Lagos.	

FEDERAL RADIO CORPORATION – FM STATIONS NIGERIA

S/N	NAME OF RADIO STATION	ADDRESS	BROADCASTING FREQUENCY
1.	Kapital FM, Abuja	Radio House, Garki Abuja.	FM (92.9 MHz
2.	Pacesetter FM, Abia	Broadcasting House, Amakama, Umuahia, Abia State.	103.5 MHz
3.	Lighthouse FM, Adamawa	Broadcasting House, Bajabure, Yola Adamawa State.	101.5 MHz
4.	Atlantic FM, Uyo	Nsukara Offot, Uyo LGA Uyo, Akwa Ibom State.	104.5 MHz
5.	Purity FM, Awka	Enugu Onitsha Express Road, Awka LGA, Anambra State.	102.5 MHz
6.	Globe FM, Bauchi	Yelwa Area, Off Das Rd, Bauchi, Bauchi State.	98.5 MHz
7.	Creek FM, Yenegoa	Adjacent to Commissioners' Housing Estate,Yenagoa, Bayelsa State.	101.5 MHz
8.	Harvest FM, Makurdi	Km16, Makurdi Oturkpo Road, Adjacent Abiam LGA, Benue State.	103.5 MHz

Appendices

S/N	NAME OF RADIO STATION	ADDRESS	BROADCASTING FREQUENCY
9.	Peace FM, Maiduguri	Damboa Rd, Maiduguri, Borno State.	102.5 MHz
10.	Paradise FM, Calabar	Ikot Effanga Mkpa, Calabar Municipality, Cross River State.	99.5 MHz
11.	Charity FM, Asaba	Asaba, Delta State.	104.4 MHz
12.	Unity FM, Abakaliki	Broadcasting House Abakaliki, Ebonyi State.	101.5 MHz
13.	Bronze FM, Benin	Aduwawa Ikpoba Hill, Along Auchi Road, Edo State.	101.5 MHz
14.	Progress FM, Ado-Ekiti	Iworoko Village, Along Iworoko Road, Ado-Ekiti, Ekiti State .	100.5 MHz
15.	Coal City FM, Enugu	Enugu, Enugu State.	92.85MHz
16.	Gift FM, Jalingo	Jalingo GRA Bypass, Jalingo, Taraba State.	104.5 MHz
17.	Jewel FM, Gombe	Gombe by-pass, Off Dukku Road, Gombe.	103.5MHz
18.	Heartland FM, Owerri	Broadcasting House,, Azaraegbelu, Owerri North LGA.	100.5MHz

S/N	RADIO STATION NAME	ADDRESS	BROADCASTING FREQUENCY
19.	Horizon FM, Dutse	Along Kujawa – Dutse Road, Near the Kujawa Housing Estate, Dutse, Jigawa State.	100.5 MHz
20.	Supreme FM, Kaduna	No. 7 Yakubu Gowon Way, Kaduna.	96.1 MHz
21.	Pyramid FM, Kano	Kano Madobi Rd, Madobi LGA, Kano State.	103.5 MHz
22.	Companion FM, Katsina	Along Katsina-Batsari Road, Near Batsari LG Secretariat, Katsina State.	104.5 MHz
23.	Equity FM, Birnni Kebbi	Along Birnin Kebbi/Kalgo LGA, Birnin Kebbi.	103.5 MHz
24.	Harmony FM, Ilorin	Along Ilorin Lokoja Highway, Idofian, Kwara State	103.5 MHz
25.	Pride FM, Gusau	Within Federal College of Education, Gusau, Zamfara State.	102.5 MHz
26.	Premier FM, Ibadan	Oba Adebimpe Road, Dugbe, Ibadan, Oyo State.	93.5 MHz
27.	Highland FM, Jos	NTA TV College, Ray Field, Jos, Plateau State.	101.5 MHz
28.	Treasure FM, Port-Harcourt	NTA Compound, Choba Road, Port Harcourt, River State.	98.5 MHz

S/N	NAME OF RADIO STATION	ADDRESS	BROADCASTING FREQUENCY
29.	Sunshine FM, Potiskum	Within NTA Grounds, Along Potiskum Road, Damaturu, Yobe State.	104.5 MHz
30.	Royal FM, Gusau	Off Sokoto - Gusau Road, Premises of Sokoto River Basin Authority, Sokoto.	101.5 MHz
31.	Paramount FM, Abeokuta	Oke Mosan along Kobape Rd, Abeokuta, Ogun State.	94.5 MHz
32.	Positive FM, Akure	Along Ondo-Akure Rd, Oke, Isikan Information Village, Akure, Ondo State.	102.5 MHz
33.	Power FM, Minna	Along Bida – Badegi Rd, Niger State	100.5 MHz
34.	Metro FM, Lagos	Broadcasting House, Ikoyi, Lagos.	97.6 MHz
35.	Progress FM, Ado Ekiti	Iworoko Village, Along Iworoko Road, Ado-Ekiti, Ekiti State.	100.5 MHz
36.	Gold FM, Ilesha	Off Iloko Road, By New Ilesha-Akure Expressway, Ilesha, Osun State.	95.5 MHz
37.	Solid FM, Lafia	Along Akurba Shendan Road, Lafia LGA, Nasarawa State.	102.5 MHz

LIST OF STATE-OWNED RADIO STATIONS NIGERIA

S/N	NAME OF RADIO STATION	ADDRESS	BROADCASTING FREQUENCY
1.	Aso FM	Katampe Hill	93.5 MHz
2.	Broadcasting Corporation of Abia State	Broadcasting House, New Station Layout, Umuahia, Abia State.	88.1 MHz
3.	Adamawa Broadcasting Corporation	Broadcasting House Complex, Hore Ladde Layout.	95.77 MHz-FM
4.	Akwa Ibom Broadcasting Corporation	No. 3, Udo Udoma Avenue Road, Off Aka Junction, Uyo.	90.5 MHz
5.	Anambra Broadcasting Service (Radio)	Enugu/Onitsha Express Road, Awka Ugwuawovu Enugu-Ukwu.	88.5 MHz FM, 10.60 KHz AM
6.	Bauchi Radio Corporation	Broadcasting House, Ahmadu Bello Way, Bauchi.	990 KHz, 846 KHz, 94.47 MHz
7.	Bayelsa State Broadcasting Corporation	Radio Bayelsa	97.1 MHz
8.	Benue Radio	Makurdi, Benue State.	918KHZ-AM, 95.0MHZ-FM

S/N	RADIO STATION NAME	ADDRESS	BROADCASTING FREQUENCY
9.	Borno State Radio	Broadcasting House, Shehu Laminu Way.	-
10.	Cross River State Broadcasting Corporation	Broadcasting House, IBB Way.	92.678 MHz, 1134 KHz (AM)
11.	Cross River State Broadcasting Corporation	Broadcasting House Old Government Field, Opposite Metropolitan Hotel, Ikom.	89.926 MHz
12.	Delta State Broadcasting Service (Asaba) Voice of Delta	Broadcasting House, Off Okpanam Road, Asaba, Delta State.	97.92 MHz
13.	Delta State Broadcasting Service (Warri) Melody FM	Warri, Delta State	88.6 MHz FM
14.	Edo State Broadcasting Service	Benin Auchi Road, Aduwawa, Benin City.	95.75 MHz
15.	Broadcasting Service of Ekiti State	Okeyinmi Street, Ilokun Road, Old Ado Local Government Secretariat.	91.5 MHz-FM
16.	Enugu State Broadcasting Service	Broadcasting House, Enugu.	96.1 MHz

S/N	RADIO STATION NAME	ADDRESS	BROADCASTING FREQUENCY
17.	Ebonyi Broadcasting Service (EBBS)	Ebonyi Television, Nkaliki Road, Abakaliki, c/o Min. of Information and Culture, Govt House Annex.	98.10 MHz
18.	Gombe Media Corporation	Broadcasting House, Buhari Estate Road, GRA.	1404 KHz-AM, 91.9 MHz
19.	Imo Broad-casting Corpo-ration (IBC)	Egbu Road, Owerri, Imo State.	AM-721kHz 416 metres; FM-94.4MHz.
20.	Jigawa State Radio	Broadcasting House, Sani Abacha Way, Dutse.	1026KHZ MW
21.	Kaduna State Media Services	Broadcasting House, No 1. Wurno, Off Rabah Road.	639 KHZ, 90.8 MHz.
22.	Kano State Radio Corporation	No 3 Ibrahim Taiwo Rd, Kano.	549KHz, 729 KHz-AM
23.	Katsina State Radio Service.	Radio House, Ibadan Street, Sabon Layi, Katsina.	9772KHZ
24.	Kebbi Broad-casting Corpo-ration (Radio)	KM 8, Kalgo Road.	945.801 MHz
25.	Kogi Broadcasting Corporation	1, Danladi Zakari Road.	94MHz

S/N	RADIO STATION NAME	ADDRESS	BROADCASTING FREQUENCY
26.	Radio Kwara	Broadcasting House, Police Road, Ilorin.	612Khz 490 Metre Band, 99.00 MHz
27.	Lagos State Broadcasting Corporation	1 SDPC House, Lateef Jakande Road Agidingbi, Ikeja, Lagos.	89.75MHz; Radio Lagos: 107.5MHz
28.	Nasarawa Broadcasting Service	Tudun Kauri, Makurdi Road, Lafia.	97.1MHz
29.	Niger Media Broadcasting Corporation	Radio House, Ibrahim Babangida Street, Niger State.	75.6 KHz
30.	Crystal FM Minna	Broadcasting House, Maitumbi, Minna, Niger State.	91.2 MHz FM
31.	Ogun State Broadcasting Corporation	Gateway Broadcasting House, KM 9, Olabisi Onabanjo Way, Ajebo Road,Ogun State.	OGBC I 603 MHz MW, OGBC II 90.5 MHz FM
32.	Ondo State Radiovision Corporation	Broadcasting House, Oba Ile, Akure.	–
33.	Osun State Broadcasting Corporation	Ile Awiye, Oke Baale, Osogbo, Osun State.	104.5 MHz, 89.5 MHz
34.	Broadcasting Corporation of Oyo State (BCOS)	Agodi Post Office, Ile Akede, Orita Bashorun, Ibadan, Oyo State.	795MHz-AM, 98.5MHz-FM

S/N	RADIO STATION NAME	ADDRESS	BROADCASTING FREQUENCY
35.	Plateau Radio Corporation	No. 5, Joseph Gomwalk Road, Jos.	313MHz in 228metre Band, 88.636-FM
36.	Taraba State Broadcasting Service (TSBS) AM & FM	Broadcasting House, 39, Barde Way,Taraba State.	1260 KHz in MWB and, 90.65 MHz FM
37.	Rivers State Broadcasting Corporation	4, Degema Street, Port Harcourt, Rivers State.	–
38.	Solid FM	Along Akoba Shendam Rd, Lafia, Nasarawa State.	102.5MHz
39.	Sokoto State Media Corporation Rima Radio	Sokoto State	540 KHz
40.	Yobe Broadcasting Corporation	Km 6, Gujba Road, Damaturu, Yobe State.	801 KHz
41.	Zamfara State Radio Service	Mal. Yahaya Secretariat, Off Zaria Road, Gusau.	–

Appendices

LIST OF PRIVATE RADIO STATIONS NIGERIA

S/N	RADIO STATION NAME	ADDRESS	BROADCASTING FREQUENCY
1.	Brilla FM (Sports)	Eleganza 634, Adeyemo Alakija House, Victoria Island, Lagos.	88.9 MHz FM
2.	Steam Broadcasting (Cool FM)	267A, Etim Inyang Crescent, Victoria Island. Lagos.	96.9 MHz FM
3.	STEAM Broadcasting (Cool FM)	1421, Independence Avenue, South City Centre, Federal Capital Territory, Abuja.	96.9 MHz FM
4.	Independent Radio	Glass House, Airport Road, Benin City.	92.3 MHz
5.	Jeremi Radio	No. 60, Effurun/Sapele Road, Ecobank Building (5th Floor), Effurun-Uvwie LGA, Warri, Delta State.	–
6.	Ceuna Communications. (Cosmo FM)	Plot 18, Pocket Estate, Independence Layout, Enugu.	105.5 MHz
7.	Minaj Systems Radio	Radio vision Plaza, Minaj Drive, Mike Ajegbo Road, Obosi, Anambra State.	89.4 MHz
8.	Ray power I and II FM	Daar Communications Ltd., AIT Road, Ilapo Village, Alagbado, Lagos.	100.5MHz FM,

265

S/N	RADIO STATION NAME	ADDRESS	BROADCASTING FREQUENCY
9.	Silverbird Communications Limited	10 Force Avenue, By Govt. House Drive, Old GRA, Port Harcourt.	93.7 FM
10.	Silverbird Communications Limited	Silverbird Communications Ltd, 17A, Commercial Avenue, Yaba, Lagos.	93.7 FM
11.	Silverbird Communications Limited	Rhythm Hall, G Series, Karu New Extension Layout, Plot 96, Flat 5, Uyo Street, Area 2, Garki, Abuja.	–
12.	Star FM (Murhi International)	MITV Plaza, Obafemi Awolowo Way, Alausa Secretariat, Ikeja, Lagos.	101.5
13.	Nagarta Radio	Kaduna-Zaria Express way, Katabu-Mararaban Jos, Kaduna.	–
14.	Love (Former Crowther) FM	No. 26, Tamale Street , By Mathematical Centre, Wuse Zone 3, Abuja.	104.5 MHz
15.	Freedom Radio	Freedom House, Sharada Industrial Layout, Phase 11, Kano.	99.5 MHz
16.	Hot FM	TSM House, Apo Hill, Gudu District, Abuja.	98.3 MHz
17.	Vision FM	Hafsat Plaza, Central Business Area, Abuja.	92.1 MHz

S/N	RADIO STATION NAME	ADDRESS	BROADCASTING FREQUENCY
18.	Zuma FM	KM 2, Minna Road, Maje High Point.	88.5MHz
19.	Kiss FM	147, Adetokunbo Ademola Crescent, Wuse 11, Abuja.	99.9 MHz
20.	Grace FM	Rakiya Ogbeha Place, 35, Mount Patti Road, Lokoja	–
21.	Okin FM	2, Bayo Oyelola Street, Offa, Kwara State.	105.7MHz
22.	Globe Broad-casting (Wazobia FM)	267A, Etim Inyang Crescent, Victoria Island Annex, Lagos.	96.9 MHz FM
23.	Steam Broadcasting (Cool FM)	Km. 16, East-West Highway, Near Syringe Factory, Rumosi, Port Harcourt, Rivers State.	–
24.	Steam Broadcasting (Wazobia FM)	Km. 16, East-West Highway, Near Syringe, Factory, Rumosi, Port-Harcourt, Rivers State.	95.9 MHz FM

NIGERIAN TELEVISION AUTHORITY (NTA)

NTA National Headquarters
Ayangba Street, Area 11, Garki
P.M.B. 113, Abuja
Tel: 234 9 2345907, 2345915
Fax: 234 9 2345914

HEADQUARTERS AND NETWORK CENTRES

S/N	COMPANY'S NAME	FREQUENCY	ADDRESS
1.	NTA CHANNEL 6, ABA	187.75 MHz	Television House, Ikot Ikpene Road, Ogbor Hill, Aba.
2.	NTA ABAKALIKI	43MHz	Enugu/Abakaliki Highway, Abakaliki, Ebonyi State.
3.	NTA CHANNEL 12 ABEOKUTA	224.25 MHz Channel 12 VHF	Oke-Egunya, P.M.B. 2190, Abeokuta, Ogun State.
4.	NTA ABUJA	567.25 MHz Channel 5	Old Parade Ground, Opp. Radio House, Area 10, Garki P.M.B. 55, Garki Abuja.
5.	NTA PLUS	471 MHz Channel 21	Old Parade Ground, Area 11, Garki, P.M.B. 55, Garki, Abuja.
6.	NTA ADO-EKITI	Channel 5	Television House, Bola Ige Drive, by New Iyin/Ilawe Road, Oke Ila, Ado Ekiti.
7.	NTA AKURE	Channel 11 VHF	Oba-Ile, Akure P.M.B. 794

S/N	COMPANY'S NAME	FREQUENCY	ADDRESS
8.	NTA ASABA	Channel II VHF	Okpanan Road, By State Secretariat Asaba, Delta State P.M.B. 5083, Asaba, Delta State.
9.	NTA AUCHI	–	Non Operational
10.	NTA AWKA	UHF Channel 5	KM 1, Enugu Agidi Road, Awka
11.	NTA, BAUCHI	208 Mhz	Television House, Maiduguri Road, Bauchi, P.M.B. 0146, Bauchi.
12.	NTA BENIN NTA	189.25 MH3 Channel 7 VHF 194.75 Mh3	West Circular Road, P.M.B. 1117, Benin City, Edo State.
13.	CALABAR	203.25 - 208.75 MHz VHF Channel 9	Murtala Muhammed Highway, Calabar.
14.	NTA DAMATURU	Y175.25 Mhz, S179.75 Mhz	Television Village, P.M.B. 1021, Potiskum Road, Damaturu, Yobe State.
15.	NTA DUTSE	Channel 10	Sani Abacha Way, Dutse Jigawa.
16.	NTA ENUGU ZONAL NETWORK CENTRE	8 VHF	Television House, Independence Layout PMB 1530, Enugu.
17.	NTA GOMBE	Channel 5, MHz 175.25	KM 8, Bauchi Road, Gombe, P.M.B. 0129, Gombe State.

S/N	COMPANY'S NAME	FREQUENCY	ADDRESS
18.	NTA GUSAU	Channel 9 VHF 522	NTA Gusau, Zaria Road, P.O.Box 1108, Samaru Road, Gusau.
19.	NTA IBADAN	108.25 MHz Channel 7 VHF Band III	P.O.Box 1460, Agodi, Ibadan, Oyo State.
20.	NTA IJEBU-ODE	814.25 MHz Channel 63 UHF	Erunmu road, GRA, Ijebu-Ode, Ogun State.
21.	NTA IKARE	–	Non Operational
22.	NTA ILE-IFE	622.25 MHz Channel 39 UHF	NTA, Oke Oloyinbo, Mokuro Road, Off More, P.M.B. 5510, Ile Ife.
23.	NTA IRUEKPEN	Channel 45 UHF	NTA Iruekpen, Ireken, Edo State.
24.	NTA JALINGO	182 MHz	Television House Mountain Jalingo, P.M.B. 1102, Jalingo.
25.	NTA, JOS	189.25Mhz video, 194.75Mhz Audio	Yakubu Gowon Way, P.M.B. 2134, Jos.
26.	NTA KADUNA	CHANNEL 4 & 6	No. 7, yakubu Gowon Way, Kaduna..
27.	NTA KANO	175.25 Mhz, 180.75 Mhz	Television House, Bompai Road, Kano.

S/N	COMPANY'S NAME	FREQUENCY	ADDRESS
28.	NTA KATSINA	5 KW Channel 8	Television House, Steel Rolling Mills, Junctions Along Katsina Dutsima Rd., Katsina.
29.	NTA KEBBI STATE	Channel 39 UHF, 619.25 MHz	NTA Birnin Kebbi, Jega Road Kalgo Kebbi State.
30.	NTA 2 CHANNEL 5	175.25 MHz	Ahmadu Bello Way Victoria Island Lagos.
31.	NTA LAGOS	210.25 Mhz	Tejuoso - Sulere, Lagos.
32.	NTA MAIDUGURI	Channel 10	Damboa Road, P.M.B. 1487, Maiduguri.
33.	NTA MAKURDI NTA	210.25 Mhz	Ahmadu Bello Way, Old GRA, P.M.B. 1020441, Makurdi.
34.	OGBOMOSHO	175.25 MHz Channel 5 VHF	P.M.B. 3005, Oja Titun, Ogbomosho, Oyo State.
35.	NTA OKITIPUPA	–	Non Operational
36.	NTA OSOGBO	702.25 MHz Channel 49 UHF	NTA Oke-Pupa/Abere Along Gbongan Road, Osogbo.
37.	NTA Owerri	UHF Channel 12	New Owerri Road, Near Concord Hotel, Owerri.
38.	NTA OYO	606.25 MHz Channel 37 UHF	NTA Oyo, Oke-Apitipiti, P.O. Box 252, Oyo.
39.	NTA PORT-HARCOURT	210.25 MHz Sound 215.75 Mhz	NTA Choba Road, P.M.B. 5797, P/Harcourt.

S/N	COMPANY'S NAME	FREQUENCY	ADDRESS
40.	NTA SAKI	224.25 MHz Channel 12 VHF	P.O. Box 383, Oke-Ado, Saki Oyo State.
41.	NTA SAPELE	–	Sapele-Benin Expressway, By Amuke Roundabout.
42.	NTA SOKOTO	62.75 MHz, 185 MHz	Garba Mohammed Road, PMB 2351, Sokoto.
43.	NTA UMUAHIA	741 Mhz	Kilometer 123, Enugu/Port Harcourt Expressway.
44.	NTA UYO	224.25 MHz Channel 12 VHF	Aka Etinan Road, P.M.B. 1188, Uyo.
45.	NTA WARRI	-	Non Operational
46.	NTA YENAGOA	-	Azikoro Road Ekiki, Yenagoa.
47.	NTA YOLA	Channel 8	No. 43, Ahmadu Bello Way, P.M.B 2197, Yola Adamawa State.

Appendices

LIST OF STATE-OWNED TELEVISION STATIONS

S/N	COMPANY'S NAME	FREQUENCY	ADDRESS
1.	ADAMAWA TV CORPO-RATION	-	Sajabare Satellite Town, Yola.
2.	AKWA-IBOM BROAD-CASTING CORPORATION TV	45 UHF	3 Udo Udoma Avenue, Uyo, Akwa Ibom State.
3.	ANAMBRA STATE BROAD-CASTING CORPORATION	27 UHF, 39 UHF	Enugu-Onitsha Expressway, Awka - Anambra State.
4.	BAUCHI STATE TV	66 UHF	Wuntin Dada, Jos Road, Bauchi.
5.	BAYELSA STATE BROAD-CASTING TV	25 UHF	PMB 36, Azikoko Road, Ekeki-Yenagoa, Bayelsa State.
6.	BENUE TV	38 UHF	PMB 10210, Makurdi, Benue State.
7.	BORNO TELEVISION CORPORATION	38 UHF	Shehu Laminu Way, Maiduguri.
8.	BROAD-CASTING CORPORATION OF ABIA STATE TV	—	PMB 7276, Umuahia - Abia State.

LIST OF STATE-OWNED TELEVISION STATIONS

S/N	COMPANY'S NAME	FREQUENCY	ADDRESS
9.	BROAD-CASTING CORPO-RATION OF OYO STATE TV	28 UHF	Ile-Akade, PMB 01, Ibadan.
10.	CROSS RIVER STATE BROAD-CASTING CORPORATION	27 UHF	Broadcasting House, IBB Way, P.M.B 1035, Calabar.
11.	DELTA BROAD-CASTING SERVICE TV	31 UHF	Off Okpanam Road, Asaba - Delta State.
12.	DELTA BROAD-CASTING SERVICE WARRI TV	41 UHF	Delta State Broadcasting House, Off Okpanam Road, Asaba, Delta State.
13.	EBONYI CABLE STATION TV	UHF 70, 72, 74	Nsugbe Hill, Abakaliki, Ebonyi State.
14.	EBONYI STATE BROAD-CASTING SERVICE TV	–	Nkaliki Road, Near State House of Assembly, Abakaliki.

LIST OF STATE-OWNED TELEVISION STATIONS

S/N	COMPANY'S NAME	FREQUENCY	ADDRESS
15.	EDO STATE BROAD- CASTING CORPO- RATION TV	55 UHF	Benin City
16.	EKITI STATE TELEVISION	–	Ilokun Village, PMB 5343, Ado Ekiti, Ekiti State.
17.	ENUGU BROAD- CASTING SERVICE TV	UHF 50	Broadcasting House, Independence Layout, Enugu.
18.	GOMBE STATE GOVERNMENT TV	91.900 Mhz	Gombe Media Corp. (TV) Broadcasting House, Gombe.
19.	IMO STATE BROAD- CASTING CORPO- RATION TV	–	Egbo Road, Owerri, Imo State.
20.	JIGAWA BROAD- CASTING CORPO- RATION TV	70, 72, 74 UHF	Radio Jigawa, Sani Abacha Way, Dutse, Jigawa State.

LIST OF STATE-OWNED TELEVISION STATIONS

S/N	COMPANY'S NAME	FREQUENCY	ADDRESS
21.	KADUNA STATE MEDIA CORPO-RATION TV	UHF 29	Wurno/Rabbah Road, Braodcasting House, PMB 2013, Kaduna.
22.	KANO BROAD-CASTING CORPO-RATION TV	UHF 67	Broadcasting House, Maiduguri Road, P.O. Box 1009, Kano.
23.	KATSINA STATE BROAD-CASTING TV	–	Television House, P.M.B 3163 Katsina State.
24.	KEBBI STATE BROAD-CASTING SERVICE	–	Kalgo Road, Birni Kebbi, Kebbi State.
25.	KWARA STATE BROAD-CASTING CORPO-RATION	25 UHF	Television House, Akpata Yakubu, PMB 1520, Ilorin.
26.	LAGOS STATE TV	–	Lateef Jakande Road, Agidingbi, Ikeja Lagos.

LIST OF STATE-OWNED TELEVISION STATIONS

S/N	COMPANY'S NAME	FREQUENCY	ADDRESS
27.	SOKOTO STATE TV	UHF 25	Rima Road, Television House, Sokoto.
28.	NASARAWA STATE BROAD-CASTING SERVICE TV	UHF 40, Keffi UHF 23	Tudun Kauri, Markundi Road, PMB 97, Lafia, Nasarawa State.
29.	NIGER STATE MEDIA CORPO-RATION	–	Broadcasting House, Minna, Niger State.
30.	OGUN STATE TELEVISION	UHF 25	Gateway Television, Abeokuta, Ogun State.
31.	ONDO RADIO VISION CORP. TV	22 UHF	Broadcasting House, Oba Ile-Akure, Ondo State.
32.	OSUN STATE BROAD-CASTING CORPO-RATION TV	22 UHF, 104.5 FM 88.65, 32 UF	K4 Ibokun Road, Ile Awoye, Oke-Baale, Osogbo.

LIST OF STATE-OWNED TELEVISION STATIONS

S/N	COMPANY'S NAME	FREQUENCY	ADDRESS
33.	OYO STATE BROAD-CASTING CORP TV	–	Oyo State, Ile Akede Orita Bashorun, Ibadan, Oyo State.
34.	RIVER STATE BROAD-CASTING CORPO-RATION TV	22 UHF	RSTV Complex, 202 Old Refinery Road, Elelenwo, PMB 5139, Port Harcourt, River State.
35.	TARABA TELEVISION CORPO-RATION	22 UHF, 25 UHF	Broadcasting House, PMB 1038, Taraba State.
36.	ZAMFARA STATE TV	694-702 Mhz	Zamfara Television Services, Opposite Gusau Central Market, Zamfara State.

Appendices

LIST OF PRIVATE TELEVISION STATIONS IN NIGERIA

S/N	COMPANY'S NAME	FREQUENCY	ADDRESS
1.	Murhi International Nig Ltd	UHF 43	MITV Plaza Obafemi Awolowo Way Alausa Secretariat Ikeja Lagos LGA,Ikeja Lagos.
2.	Universal Broadcasting Services Limited (Super Screen)	66.25 MHz, Channel: 45UH	CITI Trust Plaza 9/11 Catholic Street, Lagos.
3.	Channels Television	614.60 MHz, Channel: 39UHF	376, Ikorodu Road, Krestal Laurel House, Maryland, Lagos.
4.	Desmims Independent Television	607 MHz, Channel: 38UHF	Sheik Ibrahim Arab Broadcasting House No. 4A, Sokoto 607
5.	GALAXY TELEVISION	UHF 27	No 25 Community Road Allen Avenue Ikeja, Lagos. LGA: Onigbongbon, Lagos.
6.	DBN TV - LAGOS	Lekki Phase 1- Lagos	–
7.	Independent Television	479.25 MHz Channel: 22 UHF	Glass House, Airport Road.

LIST OF PRIVATE TELEVISION STATIONS IN NIGERIA

S/N	COMPANY'S NAME	FREQUENCY	ADDRESS
8.	Minaj Broadcast International	631.10 MHz. Channel 41UHF	130/132 Ladipo Street Matori, Mushin, Lagos.
9.	Africa Independent Television (AIT)	535.20 MHz Channel: 31 UHF.	1, Ladi Lawal Drive, Kpaduma, Hill, Abuja.
10.	SILVERBIRD TV	–	17A Commercial Avenue, Sabo Yaba, Lagos.
11.	TVC: TELEVISION CONTINENTAL	–	No 19 Alade Lola Street, Ikosi-Ketu, Lagos. LGA: Ikosi Isheri, Lagos.
12.	SUPER-SCREEN UHF 45	UHF 45	151, Ikorodu Road Onipanu, Lagos.

References

Aihe, O. (2008, June 11) HDTV: Nigeria begins digital broadcast journey.

Asobie H.A. (2012):Resource Curse and Nigeria's Development: The Missing Link, 14th Convocation Lecture of Enugu State University.

Baran, S.J. (2010). Introduction to Mass Communication, Media Literacy and Culture (6th ed.). New York: McGraw-Hill.

BBC (2008). Nigeria satellite fails in space. Retrieved on 04/08/2010 from http://www.news.bbc.co.uk/2/hi/Africa.

Bunshak, T.(2006, April – June). Digital Broadcasting is Now. NBC News: 8(2).

Channels TV.: Sunrise Daily, Lagos (January 28, 2014)

Dokpesi, J.R.(2009). "We are changing broadcasting in Nigeria.

Dominick, J.R. (2009). The Dynamics of Mass Communication: Media in the Digital Age (10th ed.). New York: McGraw-Hill.

Ekeh, D. (2009). Nigeria Television at 50: Challenge of digitization. Retrieved on 27/7/10, fromhttp://www. tvnews.com/articles_comment/ekehdesmond.html

Encarta (2008). 1998: Television: First digital broadcasts are transmitted. Microsoft Encarta Encyclopaedia: Microsoft Corporation.

Goddie Ofose: Is 2015 digital broadcast deadline realistic?-/Lagos – *Daily Independent.*

Guy, Berger (2011): Twenty Years after the Windhoek, *Declaration on Press Freedom,* Cape Town Publications.

Hanson, R.E. (2005), Mass Communication: Living in a Media World. New York: McGraw-Hill.Ibulubo, T.G.(2008). Nigeria to switch to digital broadcasting. Retrieved on 24/7/10 fromhttp://www.africanews. com/site/nigeria_to_switch

Leadership Newspapers.: INEC Advertorials on 2015 General Elections –Wednesday, January, 29th, 2014.

Mac, Bride S. : Many Voices, One World Communication and Society Today and Tomorrow: University of Ibadan Press.

Mishkind, B.(2009). The Television History. Retrieved on 03/08/10 from http://www.oldradio.com/ current/ bc.tv.htm

New Media and Mass Communication www.iiste.org ISSN 2224-3267 (Paper) ISSN 2224-3275 (Online)Vol 5, 2012.

Nuhu, Yusuf (2009): Sustaining Radio Nigeria Professional in New Delivering - The Way Forward. A Presentation of Heads of News Summit, Kano.

Ocholi, D. (2009, August 16). A new dawn in the broadcast industry" Newswatch.

Orji Ogbonnaya (2012): Memoirs of Sydney, A Publication On Open Audit Magazine December 2012.

Orji,Ogbonnaya Orji (2002): The Day Abacha Died, *Inside Aso Rock*, Spectrum Books, Ibadan .

Okpanachi, S.O.M.(2008, January). Radio Development: The case of Radio Nigeria. Paper Presented at the 2008 Commonwealth Broadcasting Association Conference; Nassau, Bahamas.Robinson, M. (Ed.) (2004).Chambers 21st century dictionary; (rev.ed.). Edinburgh: Chambers Harap Publishers Ltd.

Oshodin, D. (2009). Nigeria's digital migration a mirage? Retrieved on 27/07/10 from http://www. biz-community. com/articles/157/66/39687.html

Pate U. Retheuling- Bayero University, Kano (2007): The New World Information and Communication Order in the Era of Globalisation.

Punch Newspapers: Media Personality Profile, February 2014 Pg. 24

Radio Nigeria: Eagles Square,2003-2004 series. www.nbc.gov.ng: The Nigerian Broadcasting Commission of Nigeria .

Retrieved on 27/07/10 from http://www. modernghana. com/movie/2594/1/ are-changing.html

Rodman, G. (2006):Mass media in a changing world: History, industry, controversy. New York: McGraw-Hill.

Sachs, J.- The Penguin Press (2008): Commonwealth, Http://www.sbear.uca.edu/research/2001: Information Technology & Development .

Udeorah, B. (2008, July-September):Setting the Roadmap to Digitization. NBC News: 11(3)Uzor, B. (2008). Experts draw out roadmap for digital migration in Nigeria. Retrieved on 27/07/10 fromhttp://www. businessdayonline.com/index.php

Vanguard news Retrieved on 28/07/10 from http.//www. odilinet.com/news/source/june/11/315.html.

Wiki, (2010). Digital broadcasting history: Retrieved on 03/ 08/2010 fromhttp://www.wiki.yacapaca.com/ index.php/digital.

Index

288

Garki 5, 255, 266, 268
General Abubakar 167
General Ike Nwachukwu 101, 103-4
General Manager 43-4
General Manager of Radio Nigeria 2
General Sani Abacha 54-6, 118
generation 41, 64-5, 148, 177
Geneva 187, 189, 191
Gigginya Hotel 82-3
glamour 109, 111, 116
goal 26, 34, 48, 50
Gombe 257, 269, 275
governance xvii, 17, 26, 71, 130, 132, 161, 202, 216, 232
governance issues 216
government xv-xvi, 56, 60, 102-3, 154, 156, 161-2, 181, 185, 194-5, 198-201, 203, 231, 246-7, 250
    arms of 89
Government House 112
Government House Lagos State 61
government news 203
Governor 112-13
Governor of Enugu State on Media Relations 43
governors 41, 100, 112-13
Governor's daughter 111, 113
Gracia 120-1
grades, good 2, 4
graduate reporter, young 222
grassroot xvi, 90, 154-5
grassroot audience participation programme 154
graveside 120-1
great programmes 154
    very 129
grief 119-20

group 49-50, 54-5, 111, 130, 135, 188
group lunch 168-9
growth, economic 190, 194, 196
guests 10, 85, 110, 125-8, 130, 132, 136
    first 132-3
guidelines 67, 69, 85-6
Gusau 242, 258-9, 264, 270

H

Hard News 53, 57
Hausas 154, 157-8
HD radio 209
HDTV 209, 281
Head of State 54-6, 118, 137, 167, 222
headlines 23, 101, 103, 134, 137
High Commissions 52
high-definition television 209
home 7, 12, 22, 42, 101, 117, 171, 188-9, 217, 249-50
honesty 219-20, 236
host 6-7, 81, 84, 111, 127
hotel 74, 76, 82, 84-5, 169, 187-9, 223, 251
hotel room 224
hours 17, 29-30, 76, 116, 168, 242, 245, 248
human resources issues 35
Hussein, King 118-19

I

IATA (International Air Transport Association) 98
Ibadan 17, 118, 235, 243, 255, 258, 263, 270, 274, 278, 283
IBC (Imo Broadcasting Corporation) 262

293

304

306